In Memory of Blitz

Preface

"I can't believe you're still with us. You're a special puppy. We're going to find you a good home."

I like you. I've never met anyone who could talk.

"Everyone can. They just don't know it."

But you're different. I can feel you. I can't feel everyone.

"It's only because I'm open. You can feel my heart."

I've been communicating with animals for more than a decade. My friend and teacher, Jill Estensen, showed me how to quiet and focus my energy and connect and communicate with animals on an intuitive level using their form of language—telepathy. Telepathy is one of several intuitive abilities. It's like a muscle. The more you use it, the stronger it becomes. While some people view telepathy, or the ability to connect on the intuitive level and communicate through thought, as rare or unusual, it is a trait that each of us possesses. But most people don't realize this or believe in it.

When I first started communicating with animals, it was a challenge. I strained for the smallest tidbit of information. I walled myself off in a quiet room, shut my eyes, and concentrated hard. Sometimes I wouldn't hear anything. Sometimes I would hear a message, but I wouldn't understand it. With practice, words began to come, then phrases. Sometimes I would see a picture. Sometimes it would be more of a feeling or an impression and an entire concept would become clear.

Using The Geometries of Creation, a divination deck Jill created, made it easier. If I couldn't get answers in my head, through telepathy, I would use her cards to help me understand the issue or situation.

It took years to develop my telepathic and intuitive ability, but I finally got to the point where it became easier. But there are still times when I don't hear anything. Sometimes I'm blocked. Then there are times the words come so fast it's like a waterfall of words and I can't make them out. And I don't always know whether I'm hearing the dog's "voice" or translating it to something that makes sense in my world. Sometimes people ask me if I'm making it all up. All I know is that I hear what I hear.

I'll never forget a conversation I had with my horse, Bear, not long ago. We were taking a sabbatical from dressage, and I was going to attempt to train him in the methods of Liberty Training, a playful process where the horse is free but mirrors every movement of its human. I marched purposefully toward his pasture, his black nylon halter tossed casually over my shoulder.

He lifted his head and watched me approach, black eyes intently fixed on me. I stroked his glistening white nose and said, "I'm going to teach you to do something new today."

I love how you humans think that we don't know anything until you teach it to us.

"Funny man Bear."

So what is this new thing you're going to "teach" me?

"It's called Liberty Training," I said and then explained the concept.

I find it interesting that you want to do Liberty Training.

"Why?"

Because you are so often trying to suppress my liberty. If you were truly interested in liberty, there would be no such thing as saddles, bridles, or the bits you humans use to control us.

He had a valid point. Our animal companions often do. And it's part of the lesson I wanted to share when I wrote *Finding Forever*. When Blitz, my beautiful German shepherd, died, it was months before I was emotionally ready to search for another dog. Finally, it was time, and I hoped to find one that might be like him. I discovered the Coastal German Shepherd Rescue organization and their weekly adoption events. I spent week after week, event after event searching, and I came to know the volunteers. Many became my friends. In two months, I morphed from a prospective client to a volunteer.

Little by little, the dogs eased my grief as I attempted to comfort them back. As I spent time volunteering, the dogs' stories unfolded. Some were inspiring, others sad, and others humorous. I'd share them with friends, one of whom encouraged me to write about my experiences. And so a book was born.

I have a dream. I dream that one day there will be no abuse or neglect. That one day there will be no puppy mills or backyard breeders whose only intent is profit rather than the welfare of the dogs. That one day animal shelters will be properly funded and staffed so that they are equipped to do their jobs. I dream that one day animal rescue organizations and shelters will no longer need to exist. I dream that one day everyone will be able to communicate with their animals.

It is my hope that this book and its stories inspire, educate, and raise awareness in regard to the complexity and intelligence and higher order of the animal kingdom and to what they sometimes endure at the hands of humans.

I've been deeply touched by the wisdom and dignity these dogs possess and inspired by their ability to forgive and love unconditionally in the face of ignorance, abuse, and abandonment. And I've been humbled to witness the selfless work and tireless efforts of the volunteers that comprise Coastal German Shepherd Rescue.

Animals are here to teach us. Not the other way around. If we could suspend the veil of disbelief or skepticism, open ourselves to their guidance, and follow their example, we would be rewarded beyond anything we dreamt possible.

Blitz

Blitz was my first shepherd—a stunning, big-boned boy with a huge heart and soft, loving eyes. His dramatic silver and black coat glistened when he moved. He might have had a streak of husky in him because his tail curled slightly at the end, and he talked incessantly, howling and yowling his words with a soft friendly hint of a growl. "Woowoowoowoo," was his trademark response to everything.

Solidly built, he oozed presence and authority. And while visitors needn't have feared that he'd bite, newcomers were cautious when they got out of their cars and met him for the first time. I smile thinking back to the number of times he'd greet delivery men, repairmen, and friends as they parked their cars in our driveway, inadvertently trapping them in their vehicles as he peered through the driver's window.

One warm July afternoon, he lolled on the living room carpet. "Want to go out and play tag?" I asked.

He followed me slowly to the sliding glass door that opened to a brick patio and lush lawn. He slipped quietly through the door, barely brushing my leg. Usually, he would have blown past me, practically knocking me to the ground to reach the lawn first. Usually, the word "tag" would have incited a raucous chorus of howling and yowling as he communicated his excitement. I crouched and play-bowed, pretending to lunge for him. He sauntered unenthusiastically toward the edge of the lawn and lay down. I knit my brow and cocked my head.

"Not in the mood today?" I asked.

It's hot.

"It is hot," I agreed, feeling the heat of the summer sun beating on my back. "We'll play later. Tonight maybe." I lay next to him for a moment and stroked his fur, then took his face in my hands. "You're a special boy," I whispered, surrendering to his kind eyes. I opened my heart and poured love into him and then rose to my feet. "I'll be back."

An hour later I went outside and called him. "Bliiiiitz!" I called, scanning the yard. He'd been gone for an hour. Not like him to wander. I searched the front and backyard calling continually, waiting for the soft thunder of his gallop to announce his return. Nothing. "Bliiiiitz!" Nothing. Perplexed, I wandered back into the house and down the hall to my room.

I faced a paned window smudged with dust and grime and gazed through the laced pattern of the eucalyptus leaves in the grove beyond. Then I saw it. His lifeless body splayed out on the lime-green ice plant that covered the sloping bank. It was as though he'd dropped in midstride.

My hand flew to my mouth, and I froze at the window in shock. Then I paced back and forth, hand to my mouth still, looking for my flip-flops or any shoes I could throw on. Like a hamster on a wheel, I kept pacing, unable to break my pattern. My mind blanked. Then my throat knotted, and I doubled over, gripping chunks of hair in clenched fists. I let out a silent scream. Moments later, my head cleared, I found shoes and walked out to where he lay.

I knelt over his dead body, caressing his still warm coat. Tears welled, and my throat tightened. I rocked slightly, back and forth, like someone in a trance, only dimly aware of tears streaming down my face. Dimly aware of the sound of my sobs and my chest jerking. Dimly aware of the ice plant crushed under my weight, its juices bleeding into the denim knees of my blue jeans. I lowered my head to his side and caressed him with my cheek.

My neighbor, a vet, saw me crouching over him and jogged over.

"What happened?" he asked. He knelt beside me.

"I don't know. I just found him." I tensed my jaw to fight the tears, but they continued to fall. "He seemed off this morning, but not that bad. This feels...like the same thing...that happened when Buddy died." My sobs blocked the words. "Cancer ...of the spleen. One day... they're fine. The next...they're not." I continued rocking.

"You could be right." He put his arm around my shoulder and steadied me. "It's hard to detect. If it's any comfort, there isn't much pain with that form of cancer." We stood, and he hugged me. "I'm sorry," he said, "We all loved him. Can I help you? Bury him I mean."

"No. Thank you," I said through my tears. "I need to be alone with the kids when I do it."

We parted ways. His words haunted me. *If it's any comfort, there isn't much pain with that form of cancer.* No pain. For the animal that is. My painful journey was just beginning.

Before we found Blitz, we'd spent months looking for an older puppy. We wanted one that was between six and twelve months old. It was a compromise I'd made with my son. He'd wanted a young puppy. But we weren't home enough. To get a six-week-old puppy would have been akin to leaving an infant home all day to fend for itself.

We'd combed classified ads diligently. But each time we called on what seemed like the perfect dog, we'd be too late.

"Everything happens for a reason," I'd tell Caden. "It wasn't the right dog for us. You'll see. The perfect dog will come in time."

One day I went to see a friend at his ranch. He had eight or so dogs, a happy, eclectic pack of exotic mixes and purebreds. He led me down to the barn and pulled a heavy stall door open, leaning into it to use his body weight as leverage. A darling silver and black German shepherd bounded out like a little deer.

"I wanted him to be a surprise," he said. "I thought maybe he could be Caden's new dog."

"Oh my God! He's adorable. Where did you find him?"

"At the soccer fields yesterday in La Jolla. Someone just abandoned him. I couldn't leave him."

"Who in their right mind would abandon a dog like this? He's gorgeous."

"It happens all the time."

I took Caden to meet Blitz. Blitz jumped into his arms and licked his face. It was love at first sight.

Dogs are pack animals and, like most of the animal kingdom, are prone to travel in groups or herds. Pecking order is key to averting chaos and anarchy. Each animal has its place in the group, established through a deliberate dance of dominance and submission. The leader is called alpha. Blitz was alpha, so we had to work to make him understand that with humans, canine alpha isn't appropriate.

Like many shepherds, Blitz had a prey drive—an instinct to hunt and kill. Some dogs are more focused on wild animals, some on herd animals like sheep. Others will hunt anything that moves. Blitz was the latter, and our home in the country was a dream come true for him. He chased it all—rabbits, squirrels, birds, gophers, bees. And cats. I yelled "No!" every time he lit out after Tigger, our little female tiger cat. But it did no good.

Tigger was a tiny but fierce adversary. She'd charge him, fur bristled, claws ready, and teeth bared. If we were close by, he'd back off. If not, she'd dash up a tree or jump onto a shelf or anything high enough to be safe. It took all of our efforts—me, the kids, and Tigger. Finally, after five years of training, he stopped chasing her.

But he continued chasing everything else. In our neighborhood, most homes came with acres of unfenced land, offering a veritable playground for any dog with a prey drive. Blitz was in heaven, hunting bunnies, squirrels, and birds. I'd even tease him when he brought one home, placing a limp little rodent on his outdoor bed.

"Did you play too hard with you new little friend?" I'd ask.

But when he targeted the neighbor's livestock, it wasn't funny. He killed chickens and raced around pastures after sheep and goats. Neighbors weren't thrilled. I put him in herding training to redirect his prey drive, to teach him to herd rather than attack or kill.

I'll never forget the look in his eyes the first time he saw a herd of sheep. Blitz sat between me and the trainer. The trainer's wife ushered the sheep into the enclosure where we stood, herding them from behind. Blitz drew himself up, sat erectly, and pricked his ears. Then he whined and licked his chops in pure wonderment.

For me?

"*Not* for you, puppy. You have to learn to work with them, not kill them."

Why?

"Because you're a domestic dog. Not a wild one. It's not appropriate for domestic dogs to kill other people's animals."

I don't understand.

"Wild canines kill to survive. They kill for food. You get fed. You don't need to kill."

But I like the chase. The thrill. It makes me feel alive.

"You'll get us into trouble if you kill. No one will like us."

No response. He focused back on the sheep.

The sheep circled us. The man held Blitz's collar then turned him loose. Blitz streaked after the sheep nipping at their haunches and racing around in sheer delight. The guy was skillful, and despite Blitz's speed, he kept him from killing the sheep. It was a beautiful thing to witness.

I took Blitz for several sessions. But the constant structure seemed to be getting to Blitz, and the guy became a bit too heavy-handed for my liking. The wonder and delight I'd seen in his eyes was gone. Play had become work. So I decided that Blitz was getting it and we would continue the obedience side of the training at home. I worked with him for a year and a half, but I never really perfected the art of recall, getting your dog to return to you from a distance when called or signaled.

Overall, the training seemed to have taken effect. Or perhaps it had more to do with the fact that the neighbor with livestock moved. Either way, Blitz never killed a domesticated animal again.

Although I'd gotten him for Caden, Blitz became my dog. Probably because he considered me to be the alpha in the home. He and I bonded over long walks, yard work, and plain old hang time. He was so connected to me that if I was working in the garden and I moved even five feet, he'd get up from his resting spot to be closer to me.

And while he loved manly things like being outside, hunting for rabbits, and patrolling our property, the sound of a gunshot (ah, country living) or a clap of thunder sent him into a panic, scrambling to cower in the safety of my arms.

Many months before Blitz died, we lost Tigger. Eventually, we got two new kittens, brothers we named Taz and Baghera. We handled the introductions slowly. After all, Blitz was still a hunter. And these guys were little. My teenage daughter, Hailey, brought him into the family room and had him lie quietly.

"Blitz, you must be good. You cannot bite or chase these guys. They're babies," I said.

Don't worry. I'm afraid to move.

The kittens circled warily around him, sniffing his fur gingerly. He lay frozen in place. The kittens relaxed and began batting at his tail. Blitz looked up at me but remained motionless. Hailey and I glanced at one another and nodded. It was a good sign. Within days, we were all happily integrated. The kittens adored Blitz, and he in turn seemed to love them.

The bond between them seemed so natural and so deep that I wondered if perhaps they weren't strangers. And since I believe in reincarnation, I wondered if possibly these kittens had been with us before.

I'd been practicing animal communication for years with my own animals and often for friends and colleagues in order for them to understand their pets more deeply and address issues and problems.

Since I knew I could communicate with our new kittens, I decided to ask them. And I did what I always do when I'm trying to communicate with animals. I quieted myself, closed my eyes, and connected.

I tuned into Baghera first. "Have you been with us before?"

Yes.

Are you Boots?

No.

Sniffer?

No.

Tigger?

Yes.

"Oh my God," I said picking up the little black bundle of fluff and holding him to my heart, "Oh my God.

You've come back to us." I breathed deeply, inhaling the scent of his silken fur to capture his essence. Then I turned to Taz.

"Who are you?"

News. And Sydney.

"Really?" This was puzzling. News had been the first cat I'd had as a married woman. I adored him and was delighted to have him back. Sydney was a dog we'd had when we got Blitz. She'd passed away a few years ago. I had no idea animals crossed species when they reincarnated. I stroked his tiny back, scratched his chin, and then planted a kiss on the top of his striped head.

No wonder Blitz was being so good. He "recognized" the little guys.

When Blitz died, I didn't really grieve. I thought it was because he didn't suffer. Or that I didn't have to watch him grow old and lose his abilities. He simply went peacefully. And I thought he'd reincarnate and come back to us. While it was a shock and I missed him, I thought I was okay with it all. I was wrong. In reality, I was numb. And because his death had been a shock, I remained blocked for months.

I connected with Blitz while meditating one day. He stood strong and proud in a beautiful, sunny meadow. His coat ruffled slightly in the warm breeze.

"You crossed over safely?"

Yes. Caden helped me.

"And you are okay?"

I'm fine....there's something I need you to know.

"What?"

I came into this life to accomplish something specific. You helped me achieve a new level of consciousness in the animal kingdom.

"What does that mean?"

That I've graduated. Spiritually.

"Does that mean you'll be a different species when you come back?"

I'm not coming back.

"What!" Tears sprung to my eyes.

I don't need to. I'm done. Thank you.

He faded out, leaving me confused and saddened, his final words echoing in my ears.

I couldn't believe this. I thought he would come back. I thought he would return to our family. Now I had to face the fact that I would *never* see him again in this lifetime.

That was the first of many "nevers" that I had to come to terms with. I would never again feel his steadfast presence. Never play tag with him. Never walk with him. Never put my arm around his shoulder or hold him—ever again. It was overwhelming in the worst way. Grief welled in my chest like a tidal wave sweeping in from the sea, and I wept in the stark silence of my room.

The yard, his bed, the house, life in general—all seemed empty without him. I went through the motions of my life in a grey fog. Until Gavin came into my life. But that is another story.

I knew that Blitz had gone because he was simply ready. He'd accomplished what he'd planned to in this lifetime. It's interesting looking back that I didn't "communicate" much with Blitz. Maybe I didn't need to. Maybe we understood each other on a level that transcended even telepathy.

Animals come into our lives to serve a purpose. Sometimes they teach us lessons. Sometimes they help us process the many emotions and experiences we collect. Sometimes they help us shed the energy we take on as we help others. Blitz was all of these things. He'd been through so much with me: a divorce, several relationships since, my children growing and starting college, so many things. He was a shepherd in the true sense, and he led me through an important phase in my life.

I didn't realize when we got Taz and Baghera that it would be a catalyst for Blitz. That he would somehow know his "watch" was over and that the kittens could now take on the task of helping us. It's strange the way everything in life falls into place. There truly is a grand scheme to it all. Even if the grand scheme is painful.

It was months before I began to look for another German shepherd. My search led me to Coastal German Shepherd Rescue, and it changed my life.

Forever.

Gavin

"He's gonna have a prey drive," Hailey warned, observing Gavin's reaction to the small Pomeranian in a nearby yard. His ears pricked, and he watched the little dog intently, tracking his moves. Hailey was a good wingman and at times the voice of reason that I needed, but that day I ignored her.

I noted his prey drive, but I thought we could redirect it because we'd done it with Blitz. It had taken a while. Years actually. But I wanted Gavin, and that clouded my memory, like forgetting the pain of childbirth. And I figured since I'd done it once, the second time would be easier. I tuned into Gavin and attempted to connect.

"Do you think you could be good with cats?"

No response.

I knelt and put my arm around his shoulders. "Gavin, have you ever lived with a cat?"

No response.

"I can't get through to him. There's too much chaos here for me to connect."

"Yeah. The chaos. Right." My daughter's tone was smug.

"Yeah, yeah. I know you don't believe I can communicate with them. I can't believe you think that I'm crazy and I make all this stuff up."

"Don't feel bad, Mom. Jesus' family didn't think he was a messiah either."

"Oh my God. You kill me. Where do you come up with this stuff?" I laughed heartily. She smiled and rolled her eyes.

We walked Gavin down a partially paved road riddled with potholes. The fall sun warmed our shoulders, and a slight but dry breeze began to parch our lips and throat.

"He might be getting warm," I said resting a hand on the black saddle of his back. "We should get him back into the shade at the event."

Gavin had caught my eye almost immediately. Brand new to Coastal, Gavin was a dark-faced, black and tan, adolescent male with intense eyes and a soft, short coat. His right ear was endearingly cockeyed, tilting in just a bit. We returned to the event, and as I knelt in front of him, he licked my chin. And I was in love.

My plan that day had been to meet Legend, a beautiful classic shepherd I had seen on Coastal's website. But he wasn't at the event. Hailey and I met several dogs that day—Deuce, Archer, Bear, and Landon—but I kept coming back to Gavin. And we decided to do a foster to adopt, where you bring the dog home to see how he does before sealing the deal.

I think dogs know when they're being adopted. At least Gavin did. He dove joyfully into the collar I held out, rearing and thrusting his head through it. And he jumped into the back seat of my car without hesitation. Like he knew he was going home.

On the way home, I tried "talking" to him again. I needed him to be good with our cats. In the months since we'd brought these two wild, fuzzy little men into our home, Taz and Baghera had become beloved family members.

"Gavin, I need you to get along with the cats. You can't chase them."

I'll try.

He put his feet on the front console and eased into the front seat with me. I pushed him into the back seat. Maybe he was excited that I was talking to him and wanted to get closer. He tried again. I pushed him back again. And told him "no."

Here we go, I thought. I'd forgotten what it was like to establish rules and pecking order with a new dog—especially an alpha male. This was just the beginning.

We were home only two minutes before it was apparent that my daughter's prophecy was correct. Gavin had a prey drive. As soon as he saw the kittens, he whined and strained at the leash. I quickly ushered him out of the family room and closed the door behind us. But I adored him, and I was determined to work with him. I felt certain that this beautiful boy belonged with us and that I could train him.

I excitedly introduced Gavin to my circle of friends, boasting about our new family member to a resounding chorus of "wow"s! Everyone thought Gavin was stunning. And he was. But what I loved was how quickly he connected with me.

"Don't you love how he follows us everywhere?" I said to the kids at dinner one night.

"You mean how he follows *you* everywhere," they corrected.

They were right. Gavin and I had bonded, and I loved it. It was like having Blitz back in a younger body. When he licked my chin or leaned into my hug, my heart swelled. And yet I couldn't shake this deep sadness that welled up every time I looked at Gavin or hugged him. I thought it was just because it was all still up in the air. I didn't know if Gavin could conform. I didn't know if I could redirect his prey drive. And if I couldn't, I wouldn't be able to keep him. I just wasn't up to the stress and chaos of that kind of diligent training 24/7.

I tuned into Blitz for guidance.

"Blitz, we have this new puppy. What do you think of him?"

Never never land.

"What does that mean?"

It's not the time or the place.

Not the time or the place for what?

For any of this.

His answers confused me, so I asked more directly, "Do you think I can train Gavin? Do you think I can redirect his prey drive?"

How much time do you have?

That was clear. I knew he was telling me yes but that it would take time. Maybe a year, maybe two, maybe more. He was asking me how time I wanted to commit to this. But I wasn't ready to give up just yet.

We kept the cats tucked away in the family room and gave Gavin free rein of the rest of the house. We worked with him several times a day around the cats, using tactics we'd learned from *The Dog Whisperer*, as well as our experience with Blitz and another of our previous dogs, Sydney.

We had to keep him on the leash or hold him when one of us entered the family room where the kittens were temporarily housed. If he was free, he'd try to dash past us to get at the kittens.

When we worked with him, we'd bring him into the family room, where the cats were. We'd restrain him with a leash and ask him to sit and then lie down in their presence. If he got too alert or started tracking them with his eyes, we'd redirect him with a "shhht" sound and a slight poke at the neck to emulate a mother's teeth. If he softened, we'd praise him. If he rolled on his back and exposed his belly in complete submission, we'd lavish him with affection and assurance.

Other than his cat training, though, he was a smart boy. On the first day, he mastered "sit" and "down" with verbal commands. Within two more days, he was responding simply to hand signals. We were still working on "stay." On the fourth day, he started testing me and ignoring my commands, but consistency paid off, and on the fifth day, he was back to good behavior.

But as time passed, the only progress we'd made in regard to the kittens was that he no longer tried to blow through the door when one of us entered the family room. I began to tearfully admit that I couldn't turn this around quickly. My daughter wasn't sure either. And we'd been through this with Blitz—the awful feeling when he killed the neighbor's chickens or took off after another neighbor's goat. Of being responsible for the loss of someone else's livestock or pet. It was a lot to go through again.

My son was adamant that we not give up on Gavin.

"That's so mean," he said. "You can't bring him home and then take him back."

"Caden," I said, "I was *so* clear with him that his staying with us was contingent upon him being good with the cats."

I placed a call to Sandy, my contact at Coastal who'd introduced me to Gavin.

"We're not having much luck with the cat issue." My throat was tight.

"Yeah. I was afraid he'd have a prey drive."

"I love him, and I don't want to bring him back, but I'm not sure I can go through this again, Sandy." I began to cry.

"No. I understand."

"My son said this was mean. That we couldn't do this to him." I could barely speak. I choked out the words between sobs.

"Dobie, you can't look at it that way. You gave him a break from the kennels. And now we know far more about him and can put him in a home that's the right match. This happens sometimes, and dogs come back. It's not a big deal. Tell me what kind of home you think he should have."

I tried to regain my composure. "He has *tons* of energy. Our yard isn't fenced, so we walk him several times a day for about forty minutes. Frankly, we're all a little worn out. And he's a good boy, but he needs someone who knows what they're doing because he wants to please but he will test his people."

"So a fairly active, semi-experienced home then?" she asked.

" Yeah. I don't think most people realize how active shepherds are mentally and physically. I mean they're so intelligent, but in the wrong hands...well, you know."

"I think you're right. People don't know what they're getting into when they get a shepherd. They're not the easiest breed, although they're probably one of the most rewarding."

"Right. Gavin is sooooo smart. At first I used voice and hand commands for sit and lie down and hold. By day three, he was responding to hand commands only. But even though I'd earned his respect, he'd still test me from time to time and he'd ignore what I was asking for. I could almost feel him say, 'Did you really mean it?'"

"Yeah, some are like that at first. Especially the males."

Sandy and I laughed.

"I think if he had a fenced yard and another young dog to help him burn off steam, that would be perfect for him. And no cats." I said.

"Could you bring him to the next adoption event, and we'll see what happens?"

We hung up. But I couldn't stop crying. That night, he and I lay on the floor together, and I put my arms around him. He licked away the tears that streamed down my face. My body jerked as I sobbed, and I tried to tap into him to say goodbye.

"I'm sorry, Gavin. My beautiful puppy. I adore you."

I love you, too.

"We're going to find you the perfect home. You'll see. You'll be happier if you don't have to share your home with cats."

I want you to know something.

"What?"

You saved my life.

I sobbed even harder. "Honey, I didn't save your life," I telepathed in confusion. "Jess and Sharon, who pulled you from the shelter, they saved you."

You gave me hope.

"How?"

You gave me a home. Now I know it can happen again. I had given up hope that I could find someone like you. Someone who could talk to me. Now I know there are people like you.

We didn't say anything else. We just lay in each other's arms while I cried. Gavin and I went to the adoption event. I walked him around and introduced him to several interested couples. Sandy approached me and gave me a knowing look. She took Gavin's leash and quickly walked away. My mouth dropped open, and I watched him go. I realized she was trying to spare us both a wrenching goodbye. But the minute the leash was out of my hands, I broke down. And I started to sob again. A couple of the other volunteers hugged me, trying to comfort me.

I walked away from the event and toward my car in a daze. Part of me was relieved not to have to wage the constant vigil between Gavin and the cats. But I was still grief-stricken. I turned the key in the ignition, and tears streamed down my face. I sat there for a long time.

Through my fog, it dawned on me that I had never come to terms with losing Blitz, let alone grieved his death. I'd been shut down for months. Gavin had been put in my life as a catalyst, allowing me to process some of the emotion I'd been blocking. Losing Gavin was like losing Blitz all over again. But if I didn't grieve and let go, I'd never be whole. And so, months after losing Blitz, my grieving process finally began.

Gavin got adopted that day. To a perfect forever home. It was everything I'd dreamt for him. A fenced yard where he could romp and play. A loving couple to dote on him. A young canine "sister" to help him burn off his endless energy. And no cats.

His new family returned several weeks later to give us a glowing update on this special boy. He's doing beautifully in his new home and they adore him.

I thought about Gavin and his statement that I had given him hope. It has been said that hope is a veneer that we apply over yesterday's disappointments. I think it is far more than that. Hope is a beacon that shows us the way through dark and lonely territory. Hope is our ballast as we push boundaries and stretch beyond our own conformity. To carry hope in one's heart is to burst forth as a light to the rest of the world.

And when hope springs eternal, we are all blessed.

Klaus

"What about Klaus?" I asked.

"Oh, not for you." Sandy laughed.

"Why not?"

"He's kind of a badass. Huge prey drive…he'd eat your kitties. Besides, he's in doggie rehab."

"What does that mean?"

"It means he's started biting. So he's in training with one of our volunteers."

When I met him in person, he took my breath away. He has that effect on everyone. Klaus is a stunning, regal archetype for the German shepherd breed. One hundred pounds of muscle and sinew and thick bone cloaked in luxuriant cream, bronze, and black fur. His eyes—wild and wolf-like—command passersby to stop in their tracks.

Klaus is aloof. Like a gorgeous bachelor in a sea of desperate women, he knows that everyone wants him but that few are his equal. He plays it cool at the adoption events, observing transactions with detached air. Unless someone he takes offense to approaches his crate. Then he explodes. Like a police dog in full attack mode—settling only when his target has slunk respectfully away.

He'd been with Coastal for months while they searched for an appropriate match for him. Someone who understands how to be alpha without crushing his beautiful spirit. Someone he can look up to, respect, and protect. But as the weeks passed, no match was found.

Caron, one of Coastal's lead people, asked me one day, "Will you get into his head and figure him out?"

"I can try," I replied. I quieted myself and closed my eyes. I visualized Klaus and then I connected.

"Klaus, what's up with the biting?"

I've pretty much always been this way.

"It's not new?"

No.

"Is it why your people relinquished you?"

One of the reasons.

"Biting isn't appropriate."

I don't care.

"It hurts, Klaus."

I didn't know that.

"Were you abused?"

Yes.

"I'm sorry."

The frequency of it astonished me.

"There is much ignorance in the human race."

It is to be expected.

"It needs to change. The abuse…is that why you bite?"

One of the reasons.

"What other reasons?"

It's just so tempting.

I understood what he meant. Biting was a visceral, primal experience for him. The faint tickle of body hair. The spongy feel of the flesh giving way to meaty, taut muscle. All reminding him of his natural urge to hunt. It was simply his nature.

"If you want to live with in harmony with people, you have to stop biting," I said.

I don't care if I live with people.

"What *do* you want?"

I've pretty much had it.

"With what?"

Life. Domestication. I want to be free.

This all seemed so extreme. Was this dog telling me he was done? That he'd given up? That because he'd been abused he was unwilling to trust?

Then I doubted my intuition. What if I had heard him wrong? What if I'd misunderstood? I reported back to Caron with a caveat: "Grain of salt with all this…. I could be wrong."

One day, Klaus was adopted. And it seemed a good match. He went with strict instructions to the new people about what not to do. And we held our breath, willing this to work. Well, I didn't hold my breath. I knew it wouldn't work. His new people took him to a pet store and then let him off the leash at a dog park. Neither experience had gone well. Klaus was returned within a week.

I watched him go through his paces at event after event. Once, I caught him staring at me. Fixing me with his wild, golden eyes.

I remember you, he said.

"And I you," I replied.

You talked to me.

"Yes."

I like you.

"I'm honored."

At the adoption events, Klaus was tucked into the background in his crate to protect him and everyone else. But people are drawn to him and seek him out anyway. His wildness is a beacon for the weak or simply those cut from the same cloth. He makes it clear who's allowed near and who isn't. It's almost comical.

Especially since no one was ever hurt.

He shuttled back and forth between two fosters: Tess, our leader, and Mike, another volunteer. They are the only two people Klaus likes. I'll never forget the day he went off on me. Tess had asked me to come with her to her SUV to get some meds for one of our dogs. Klaus was inside the vehicle perched in the back seat. She opened the driver's side door. Klaus spotted me and exploded. I flinched, and even though a pane of glass separated us, my heart pounded.

"Car alarm's working," Mike quipped from a few feet away.

"You tell him I'm crushed," I replied. "Never mind. I'll tell him."

I was surprised he'd reacted so strongly since we'd connected. But he was just defending his territory.

Weeks later, my daughter and I arrived at an adoption event that was already underway. As we approached, we could hear one dog above the others, barking incessantly in a deep, resonant baritone.

"Guess who that is," I said.

"Klaus," she correctly guessed.

"Klaus, Klaus, Klaus," I admonished, shaking my head in amusement. "Not the way to get adopted, bud."

But Klaus didn't care if he got adopted. He's wild and wants to be free.

One night I had a vision of him running free in a forest. His bushy blond hindquarters pumped powerfully as he jogged away to explore his new territory. He looked more like a wolf than a dog.

The next morning, I had an epiphany. There was a wolf preserve nearby. What if I could pay for Klaus to go there? What if I could set him free?

I reached out to the wolf preserve and explained his plight. I inquired about whether they could take him to see if he could integrate with the other wolves. Their response was no. They wouldn't take him. They couldn't see my vision for him. And even if they had agreed, Coastal probably would have thought I was nuts.

I broke down and cried even though I know everything happens for a reason. If the answer was no, then it wasn't meant to be. And I had to accept that while Klaus might be wild at heart, he was *not* wild by nature. Perhaps the wolves would have welcomed him—as a meal. Which wouldn't have been in his best interests. I had considered that possibility when I reached out to the wolf preserve. That the wolves might kill him rather than coexist. I think he would have found honor in that—a warrior's death. But that isn't his destiny, so it isn't how his story played out.

Charles Lindberg once said that true freedom lies in wildness, not in civilization. Perhaps that is why Klaus remains wild at heart. Without this, the abuse of his past might have crushed him. Instead, he rises up, hearkening back to a more primal existence where life and death play out in a simple drama. He is a bold reminder that within each of us exists a spark that urges us to explore uncharted paths, to forge into unconquered territory, and to achieve our wildest dreams. A determined dichotomy of domestic and wild, Klaus reminds us that to integrate all parts of the self—wild and domestic—is to become whole.

Perhaps the vision I saw of him running wild in a forest was a premonition of something yet to come. Perhaps somewhere, there would be a home with acres of land where Klaus could integrate his heart's desire and run free.

A few months later, Tess and Mike adopted Klaus. He lives with a pack of shepherds in the country on an acre of fenced land. It was the perfect ending to his story, and I, in particular, am eternally grateful that dreams can come true. Especially for our beautiful, wild Klaus.

Legend

He had the regal, classic look I loved. Black and tan, a hint of eyeliner, and a solid, strong build. There was kindness in his eyes and pride in his stance. Legend was one of the first dogs I was drawn to when I discovered Coastal's website.

Like many of the dogs in our care, he'd been found as a stray. Wandering the streets perhaps looking for the family that had abandoned him. Coastal rescued him, and he'd been living with one of their core volunteers for about two months.

But he never attended any of the events, so I never had the chance to meet him. And I'd almost given up finding another shepherd that was good with cats. The ones I was drawn to usually came with pretty high prey drives. One day I noticed that Legend's bio had been updated by his foster mom. He was good with cats!

I placed a call and was put in touch with Caron, Legend's foster mom. Caron told me she'd already turned down at least fifteen potential families for Legend because she was waiting for the perfect home to materialize. She confided that in the short time she'd had him she had grown to love him deeply. The only reason she wasn't keeping him herself was that her female shepherd, Mandie, was bossy and bullied Legend. After our thirty-minute conversation, she felt confident that we were a match for her special boy.

We made arrangements to come early to the next event and take him before things got hectic. It was love at first sight. He was a beautiful, well-mannered boy. A gentle giant. And everything we were looking for.

When we got home, I instinctively knew he'd be good with our kitties. He was off-leash with them in ten minutes. And although he had grown to love Caron and was sad to leave her, I thought he'd adjust as time went on.

I took him to the ranch where my horse was boarded, and he behaved beautifully. Soon, he was off-leash there too. Nothing fazed this guy. Even my horse liked him. He was almost too good to be true.

Legend's only flaw was that he wasn't housebroken. He told me he didn't completely understand the concept. So we were just diligent about taking him out to potty every couple of hours to avoid an accident.

I knew that being separated from Caron would be wrenching for him, so I asked him about it.

"Do you miss her?"

I'm heartbroken. But I understand why I'm not staying with her.

"I'm sorry, sweetie. I'll do my best to help."

No response.

"Caron wants to know what you thought of Mandie."

She's a controlling witch.

I laughed.

But I was willing to put up with her in order to be with Caron. I think it bothered Caron more than it bothered me.

"Mandie's bullying you mean."

Right.

"Did you ever try talking to her?"

Mandie or Caron?

"Mandie."

I didn't see much point.

One day, out of the blue, my son told me that Legend had started growling at him as well the kittens. That seemed out of character. I emailed Caron to see if he had ever done that with her teenage son or their cats. But I knew as I sent the email that he hadn't. This was new behavior. I didn't want to lose Legend, and I needed my son to make an effort.

"Caden," I said, "I need you to try with Legend."

"He's not trying with me!"

"Honey," I implored, "he's hurting. His family abandoned him just months ago. And now he's lost Caron too. He is *not* able to rise above this on his own. And he is *not* going to be able to be the bigger person here. I need you to make an effort."

Caden did try, but it didn't work. He called me at work a few days later, proclaiming that "Mr. Wonderful" had snarled at him again.

So I tuned into Legend to figure it out.

"Legend," I said, "you are displaying the *only* behaviors that you know would cause me to have to relinquish you. And I know you've never acted out these behaviors before. What's going on?"

I want to go back with Caron.

"But Mandie was bullying you."

I told you…it bothered Caron far more than it bothered me.

"So you don't want to stay with us?"

No.

"Okay," I sighed. "I'll speak to Caron."

I called Caron and told her everything. It was a lot to absorb. I told her that in addition to Legend wanting to be with her, I felt that there was a lesson and an opportunity for Mandie in all this: to rise above her power-tripper pattern and to break the cycle of dominance that she had been using to control the household.

"Caron, you need to stop feeling guilty about Mandie's behavior. She's using your guilt to control the situation and feed her pattern."

"But it just kills me to see him slink away from her," she said. "He's too noble for this. That's why I wanted your home for him. Where he doesn't have to be bullied."

"That's not important to him," I said. I paused and then continued. "Look, I know you think my home is better for him, but Legend doesn't care about that. He loves you, and he wants to be with you. No matter what."

"But you're everything I hoped for him. Being in the country, long walks, the horses. He loves all that."

"Not as much as he loves you." I said, pausing again for a moment. "Look, let's say for the case of argument that I was in love with someone who could stand to lose a few pounds, was balding, and maybe wasn't the richest guy in the world. But I love him anyway. Then along comes Prince Charming. He's gorgeous, has all his hair and teeth, and he's rich. But none of that matters to me because I love the other guy."

"Okaaay…?"

"Well…I'm not saying that I'm Prince Charming and you're a paunchy, balding guy, but you get my point."

We giggled.

"Caron, home is where the heart is. Legend would live in a tent in Siberia to be with you. He was reborn with you. You helped to mend his fractured spirit. And for that, you will *always* have his heart. He'll never love me that way."

"All right. Hey, since you've connected with him, let me ask you something else. He has accidents in the house. Can you ask him what's up with that?" she asked.

"Oh, right. I talked to him about that already. He's not housebroken. He doesn't understand what that's all about."

"I had a feeling. But it seemed so unusual for an older dog not to be. So I was confused."

"Yeah. I pretty much let him out every hour to do his thing."

"Can you do one more thing? Could you talk to Mandie and ask her to be nice?"

"Of course. But know that she won't change overnight."

"Do you have to meet her first…or be in the same room with her?"

"No."

"Really? How do you know that you have the right dog when you tune in?"

"Trust."

"Do they ever come to you? I mean, does a dog ever

tune into you? Or do you always have to be the one that initiates the communication?"

"Generally, I have to initiate it. For a couple of reasons. One being I'm not that good yet. I'm not always in tune, like my friend Jill or people who do this for a living, animal communication I mean. Compared to them, I'm a beginner. The second reason... animals aren't used to humans having telepathic skills. So they don't seek it out in us. Once an animal knows I can communicate, they sometimes reach out. Usually, they'll pop into my head, then I'll know they're trying to connect. Or if we're in the same space, I'll notice them staring at me."

"Fascinating. Well, let me know what you find out about Mandie."

After we hung up, I quieted myself and connected with Mandie. I could see her, lying down, half asleep, her paws crossed under her chin. She could have been Legend's twin sister.

"Maaandie," I crooned, waking her ever so gently from her nap.

Mandie perked, looking for a human to attach to the voice.

"Mandie, Legend is coming back. Can you be nice to him?"

Nope.

"Mandie, I understand you consider yourself to be the queen of the household. But being the queen doesn't mean you have to rule with an iron fist. In fact, the queens people remember and revere are those that rule with dignity, and wisdom, and compassion."

Really?

"Do you think you can try that? Can you rule quietly alongside Legend?"

I don't know.

"Well, you may see a change in Legend when he comes back. He knows now that he doesn't have to be the 'perfect' dog in order to stay with Caron. So he may start standing up to you."

I withdrew my energy, leaving Mandie a little befuddled by what had happened. Then I called Caron to share the conversation.

"Tell me a little more about Mandie's background," I said.

"You don't know her whole story by now?" she teased.

I laughed. "I'm not *that* good. And we didn't go into it."

"She was a junkyard dog. Literally. Mandie and her brother guarded a junkyard."

"No kidding?"

"For the first years of their lives, they patrolled old abandoned cars, metal scrap heaps, and other people's castoffs. Until at five they became a liability and too old to be considered insurable guard dogs. So their owner faced a choice. Lose his insurance on the yard or give

Mandie and her brother up. So they came to Coastal."

"And you didn't try to adopt them together?"

"We felt it was better to separate them. He bullied her."

"Hmm."

"In fact, my daughter thinks that this is why she bullies Legend. It's the only type of relationship she knows."

"Ohhhh, that explains everything. She was never in charge before, so now she's exerting her authority. She needs to learn to balance her power. That's the lesson for her, to come from a place of compassionate authority."

After I hung up, I sat on the floor next to Legend and curled my arm around his shoulders. He leaned into me, and I steadied my body with my other arm.

"You're going home, sweet boy." Tears welled in my eyes. I was losing another one.

You are doing the right thing.

"I know. But you are special. You remind me of Blitz. I will miss you." Tears fell,

streaming down my cheeks and stinging my eyes.

There will be another. All is well. Trust your journey.

A few days later, Caron retrieved Legend, and he went back to live with her. Legend and Mandie had their ups and downs. Every so often, I "went" to Mandie to remind her of what good behavior looked like. And I remind Legend to try not to have accidents in the house. For the most part, things became more harmonious in the household.

I believe Legend was put in Mandie's life to model kindness, benevolence, and compassion. To be an evolved role model that she could emulate. Whether she follows his lead remains to be seen. If so, she will have to work hard to overcome bad habits and old patterns. If she can learn to come from the heart instead of her ego, she will be happier in the end. And she will never again feel the need to compete for attention or love.

Like most of us, Legend is a student as well a teacher. And like Mandie, he has his own lessons to learn. He's learned lessons about communicating his wishes, manifesting his heart's desire, and never giving up.

Webster defines the word "legend' as a person or thing that inspires. When I think of Legend, I remember how peaceful and harmonious it was to have him in our home. How my heart swelled each time I hugged him. How gently he kissed my cheek and chin. And how he inspired me to surrender to his soft brown eyes—the window to his deeply beautiful soul and the gentle wisdom within. I remember how, in a short time, I came to love him and felt his love in return. And how his presence helped mend a piece of my broken heart. He is aptly named—for he is a legend in his own right.

Legend passed away nine months after returning to Caron's home. Almost a year to the day after Blitz passed away. It was devastating for all of us. I know

Legend was ready to go. I know that for him, the timing was appropriate. And I know that there is a reason for everything. But it is always sad when the great ones go.

At Caron's request, I went to Legend after he passed. We didn't actually converse. It was more like an energy exchange. When I withdrew, I called Caron.

"He is completely unencumbered now that he is free of his physical body. Complete and utter freedom and a lightness that he had never felt before. Completely devoid of pain or discomfort."

"Thank you," she said.

"In our physical bodies, I think we forget even the little aches and pains we carry around. Legend had gotten used to a lot of discomfort, and the feeling he shared with me was like a spring breeze blowing through his energy. It was one of the most utterly blissful and delicious things I have ever felt. Almost like he was a sheet of fabric wafting in the breeze as it flowed through him. There was deep joy and peace connected to it. I wish you could feel it."

"I do too." She choked on the words.

"There is something more. Even though he only had a year with you, it felt like much longer. In a good way. There was so much he got to complete with you, as though the one year he spent with you was an entire lifetime to him."

Legend's last message to Caron was a lifeline for her as she came to terms with her grief, but it carried a far deeper message than simply knowing that Legend was at peace. He is a reminder that even a short period of sincere love has the power to truly heal.

At Coastal, we save their physical lives and begin the healing process. But it's their forever homes that save their spirits. It becomes a two-way street. What you put into the world comes back to you tenfold. As we help their wounded bodies and spirits to heal, that healing is reflected back to us like heat radiating from a fire. Their healing becomes ours, and they touch us at the deepest levels, sometimes healing wounds we didn't know we had. It's like the famous last line in *Pretty Woman*, when Julia Roberts says to Richard Gere, "She rescues him right back."

If Caron could look into Legend's eyes once more, her message to him would be simple.

"You rescued me too."

Kerberos

He'd told me even before I met him that he probably wouldn't be able to resist chasing a cat. Caron had sent me his photo and a brief description and asked me to communicate with him prior to the event. So I went to him.

"How are you?"

Hungry.

"For food? Or love and affection?"

Neither.

"What then?"

Knowledge. Stimulation.

"They say knowledge is power."

Whose?

"Whoever has it I suppose." I laughed, and then asked, "What kind of home do you want?"

Active.

"With kids?"

Kids are fine. Maybe older kids.

"What about cats?"

I'm not sure I like them, except to chase.

When I met him, I fell in love. I wanted him so desperately I cat-tested him anyway. As he approached their crate, our cats, Taz and Baghera, watched him nonchalantly. They knew the drill. They'd gone through this process with at least fifteen of Coastal's dogs, so they knew they were safe. I'd asked Jess to help me evaluate him. In addition to cat-testing most of the dogs, she and another volunteer, Sharon, shoulder the heartbreaking task of making the weekly runs to the shelter and deciding who can come into Coastal's care. And it devastates her to leave anyone behind.

Kerberos eyed the cats curiously and sniffed gingerly around the edges of the crate.

"That's not bad," Jess said.

But he was displaying too much curiosity for me. He'd already failed my cat test. The only ones I pass are those who show little interest and walk away. Kerberos started to whine and paw at the crate.

"Give him time. He may settle," Jess said.

I knew he wouldn't.

He pushed his nose at the metal grate on the front of the crate and scratched at the heavy plastic.

"Okay, *that's* not good," she said, pulling him off the crate. Kerberos had just failed Jess's cat test too.

But he'd find a wonderful home with someone. He was a breathtaking two-year-old male with a beautiful creamy-soft black and tan coat. And he loved people. I thought his name was interesting, given that Kerberos was the name of the mythical hound who guarded the gates of Hell. While he wasn't good with cats, he definitely wasn't scary enough to keep anyone confined within the gates of Hades. Kerberos was a love bug.

"Kerby, you're such a shweeet puppy," I'd tell him when I handled him at the events. I'd give him a hug and kiss his head and tell him we were going to find the perfect home for him.

Aside from his prey drive, Kerberos was a sensitive boy — so sensitive the only collar he would tolerate were those made of nylon webbing.

The second time I cat-tested him, I'd planned to see several other dogs. Since I had my cats and Kerberos was there, I gave him a second chance. He failed again.

"He's really not good with cats," I said to Caron when I brought him back in. She stood next to his current foster mom.

"He's good with *my* cat," his foster mom said.

I was stunned. How could that even be possible? This dog had told me he wasn't good with cats, and he'd failed two cat tests. The foster mom turned away, and I mouthed to Caron, "There's no way this dog is good with cats."

Caron told me later that day that Kerberos had been adopted. To a home in the country with chickens and rabbits. I raised my eyebrows.

"I know," she agreed. "We told them he'd chase, but they said he'd never be around the other critters."

Several weeks later, I learned that in his old foster home, he and the cat were seldom in the same room. No wonder he'd gotten along with the cat.

One day, as I sat in my office, Kerberos popped into my head. I could see his beautiful face and the way his head tilted inquisitively to one side.

"Hey, Kerby," I said. "How are things in your new home?"

My new people are mean. His tone was flat and slightly indignant.

"What's happening?"

They don't understand me.

"What do you mean?"

I'm being punished for chasing things.

This alarmed me. Was he being hurt? I emailed Caron and shared his message.

Grain of salt, I wrote, I may not have my facts straight. Plus, he's *so* sensitive that his people might just be telling him "no." That alone would feel like punishment to him. Could you reach out to his new home and see how things are going?

Caron emailed me the next day. You nailed that one, she wrote. He *is* chasing things and he *is* being told "no." But his people adore him and are working with him.

I was relieved, and suddenly his message seemed kind of humorous. Not only the message but the matter-of-fact way he'd communicated: "My new people are mean."

About a month after he'd "contacted" me, we learned that Kerby had brought his new people one of their chickens. In his jaws. Kerberos was returned the next day.

But what did they expect? You can't take an animal with a prey drive and expose him to prey on a daily basis and expect him to ignore the constant temptation. Kerberos was simply following his instincts. He probably thought he was bringing his people a present.

His situation reminded me of Blitz. I'll never forget the day my neighbor rang my doorbell and announced in a surly tone that Blitz had killed six of their chickens that morning. Until that moment, Blitz hadn't known he was a herder. I could almost feel his delight at discovering this new skill. But you can't herd chickens. They'd probably scattered, and in a frustrated attempt to keep them together, he'd opted to kill them.

It was likely that the same was true for Kerberos. He was probably delighted to find out he had a new skill and a new creative purpose. He was simply acting on instinct, being true to his inner nature. If you can see it that way—without judgment—the true beauty of the situation unfolds and you understand the behavior as part of a sequence of events that is perfectly timed—whole and flawless. And part of the beautiful and infinite cycle of life.

Kerberos got re-adopted quickly to a couple who fell in love with our beautiful boy. He sat at my feet while the new couple filled out the adoption papers, leaning against my leg. The woman commented on how connected he seemed to me. My eyes welled.

"I love him," I responded. "He reminds me of my shepherd. I lost him a few months ago."

"Will you miss him…Kerberos I mean?"

"Yes, but I'm not the right home for him."

What I didn't say was that I wasn't ready for another dog. While I had wished to find another shepherd, I was still brokenhearted. Sometimes a new relationship can heal a broken heart, and sometimes the wounds of the past must be healed first, before you can grow into your wish.

It was not Kerberos' destiny to heal my broken heart; it was his destiny to fulfill his own wish. So he moved on to his forever home. Where no temptations exist. Where he can be doted on and cherished. Where he's not constantly told "No!" And where he can have a most deserved and happy ending.

I "went" to Kerberos weeks after he was adopted and asked him how things were. He told me that he loves his new home. His new people are active, and there is always something going on. And his mind and body are always stimulated. It was exactly what he had wished for in my first conversation with him. He told me his new people are kind and that they understand him and his needs. And while he was hurt when his previous families abandoned him, he understands it was all part of the process that led him to his forever home.

Spartacus

"Wowwww!" I exclaimed. "He's amazing!"

He evokes the same reaction from everyone. Spartacus is a strapping, five-year-old sable male. Big-boned and heavily muscled, like a gladiator, he tips the scales at 120 pounds. Deep, coarse fur bristles thickly around his neck and shoulders, and his black face is strikingly juxtaposed by a pale-cream-and-grey flecked coat. Dark eyes glow green when the light hits just right, and a hint of silver sparkles on his muzzle.

Caron asked me to get a read on him before the adoption event as a possibility for our home. But he told me he wouldn't be good with cats. When I asked him why, he said that he'd like to eat them.

I don't always trust my first intuitive screening. Sometimes one dog can bleed into another, especially if there are several on the list to "profile." And I'm never 100 percent sure about the final question I always ask— "Are you good with cats?"—although I should trust it. Looking back at all the dogs I've met through Coastal, I recall being wrong about the cat issue only twice.

At the adoption event, my daughter and I fell in love with Spartacus. We cat-tested him, and he passed with flying colors. He wasn't at all interested in them. Sometimes dogs "cheat" to pass their cat test so they can get adopted into a good home. But I didn't know how to spot this. No one does.

Everyone Spartacus meets is his new best friend. He readily and joyfully shares kisses and leans into your hug in a way that endears him to you immediately. That's why my daughter and I fell in love with him. When no one adopted him that day, we decided to foster him with the intent of adopting him if he continued to be good with the cats.

Despite his size, I thought he'd be easy to handle, because he seemed so eager to please. But like many large males, he used his size to his advantage and made me earn his respect.

He'd blow past me through doors, and although it was probably part of his protective instinct, it was also his way of hanging onto his alpha status. So I'd grab his collar and redirect him back through the door admonishing, "You want to try that again?" We'd repeat this over and over until he would wait and walk through doors behind me.

I'd ask for sit and he'd eye me, testing. I'd ask again. No response. "Spartacus. Sit," I'd say firmly with a gentle hand on his haunches. Finally he'd sink reluctantly into sit. It took a couple of days for me to establish alpha with him. But he'd only been neutered a few days before he came to stay with us. With all that testosterone still in his system, you'd expect a little belligerence. It continues to astonish me that many of our dogs come to us unaltered, despite being older.

After we worked with him consistently for two days, he pretty much toed the line. Except with the cats. He wanted to get at them. Spartacus taught me to never again doubt my intuition. After that, I never cat-tested another dog. I evaluated them based only on what they "told" me.

Aside from the cat issue, he was pretty much the perfect dog. Respectful, great on a leash, a dream to walk, and excellent recall. One night I let him out to go potty, and he lit out after some prey I couldn't see. Panicked, I whistled for him to return. If I lost this dog, Coastal would kill me. He stopped in his tracks and circled back to me. To say that I was impressed was an understatement.

I think that Spartacus had been a city dog. That he'd never experienced the sights and smells and sounds of country living. Exploring our property became a favorite pastime for us. I adored how protective he was. How he followed ahead, a practice shepherds have of leading the way but looking over their shoulder every few steps to make sure you're okay. How he kept me in his sights and thundered back to my side if I changed direction, just like Blitz used to do.

Out on patrol, he looked more like a wolf than a dog. Every fiber acutely heightened to the wildness around him. Ironically, I'd probably been the one to unleash his prey drive.

I think it's possible that he'd never seen a cat before he came to our home. I remember he'd basically ignored them when we cat-tested him.

During his first face-to-face meeting with Taz, Spartacus licked him ever so gently. At first, I thought it was a good sign. But then he gingerly bit at Taz's fur like he was tasting food for an Arab sheik. Or simply sampling something new for the first time. That was *not* a good sign. Several days later, he took Baghera's head in his mouth. I pulled him off. And was more watchful in the future.

One night I came home from work wearing a fuzzy black angora sweater. Spartacus greeted me joyfully, wagging his tail furiously. Then he sniffed my sweater and began nibbling and biting at the fur. Again, it was all pretty gentle. More like curiosity than aggression. But I sensed it would escalate. I sensed that true to his word, he would eventually try to eat the cats.

We kept Spartacus separated from the cats and worked with him daily to see if we could redirect his prey drive. As time went on, my daughter and I dejectedly had to admit that while Spartacus was far more respectful of us now than he'd been on day one, he was *not* more respectful of the cats. The only reason he didn't try to get at them was because he knew he was restrained with a leash.

But we'd never be able to trust him off-leash or alone with the kittens, and it was becoming an exhausting vigil keeping everyone separated and safe. And it wasn't in his best interest to stay with us. He needed a home where he wouldn't have to be constantly schooled in cat manners. And where he wouldn't have to suppress his instincts. I reluctantly took him back to the kennels, knowing I would miss him.

What puzzled me about Spartacus was his level of neediness. He craved constant affection and reassurance. More than any dog I'd ever known. You'd expect this from a dog who'd been abandoned, but there was something different to this. We poured love into this dog, but it didn't seem to make a difference. Often, I held his face, looked deeply into his eyes and tried to fill him with love. But something was missing. I couldn't feel his heart; it was like a blank slate.

I asked him one night why his people had given him up.

I grew up. They wanted a perpetual puppy. Actually, I've had a couple of owners.

"Several owners in five years! Hard to believe."

I think they got bored.

"Is that why you're so needy?"

I want love.

"You have love. Everyone who meets you falls in love with you."

No response.

"You have to open your heart. I should know."

What do you mean?

"I lost my shepherd. And I walled off my heart for months. Then a special dog, Gavin, came into my life. He opened up the wound, and slowly I began to heal. Other dogs—Legend, Kerberos, all from Coastal—they helped me."

Are you healed?

"I think so. At least partially, or I wouldn't have been able to help you."

I withdrew and pondered our conversation. It occurred to me that Spartacus wanted a different kind of love. The kind that would never abandon him. The kind he could count on from lifetime to lifetime. Where he might even be able to reincarnate with the same family and experience the kind of bond that will give him the security he so desperately longed for. He was looking for the love of his life.

But because his heart wasn't open, no matter how much love he received, it was never enough. So he struggled to hold on to everything, hoarding every morsel of attention, yet it didn't make a difference. He simply couldn't absorb it, and he still craved more.

He hadn't learned that in order to have the kind of love he wanted he needed to open his heart again completely. No matter what. He had to learn to love as though his heart had never experienced pain or disappointment. Even though it had. I tried to tell him this, but because he was blocked, I didn't think I was getting through.

So I held the hope that he would learn that he must open his heart. If he could, he would find serenity and release the burdens and anxieties born of a lifetime of uncertainty. And I held out hope that his next home would be a home where time and love would help him heal and open his heart again. Forever.

I reinitiated with Spartacus two weeks later at an adoption event that took place on Valentine's Day. He was being handled by another volunteer, and I was taking a much-needed but short break. I knelt before him and engulfed him with open arms and an open heart. I drew back and took his face in my hands, looked deeply into his eyes and "felt" his energy.

Something had changed. Something was different.

He was truly happy to see me, not because he wanted love or attention, but because his heart was open. And now he could feel everything.

"You opened your heart!"

Yes.

"What made you decide to do it?"

You told me I wouldn't find love until I did.

"Good for you. It takes courage. You'd be surprised how many people won't do this because they fear being hurt again."

Both the day and our adoption event began winding down. A woman approached me and announced that she wanted to adopt a dog. She was a spritely thing, dressed in designer sweats and diamond earrings the size of dimes. Her eyes sparkled and her auburn hair was pulled up in a chic ponytail.

"Are they all purebreds?" she asked.

"So many are strays who find their way into the shelters that we don't know much about their pedigrees. Some look like they are. Others are clearly not. Once in a while, we get an owner turn-in and they come with papers. If pedigree is important to you, you might be better off with a reputable breeder."

"It's not. I was just asking."

"Are you looking for a male or female?"

"Female."

I showed her several females, but none seemed to do it for her. For some reason, I sensed that a male would be better for her. But I didn't know why. So I introduced her to several males. Again, none seemed to be a fit. Then Spartacus caught my eye. I put the dog I was handling in a crate, whisked Spartacus from another volunteer, and we walked outside for a meet-and-greet. I kept watch while she walked him, and when she bent to hug his shoulders, he licked her chin heartily. She adopted him on the spot.

Later that day, I followed her home to do a site visit. It was everything I'd hoped for him. A beautiful home in the country with acres of fenced land to explore. Where his people are home all day and can nurture his healing process. Where he will go for daily walks and be an integral part of the family. Where he will never again want for anything.

During the visit, I met her husband—a frail, elderly man to whom she was part wife, part nursemaid.

Suddenly, I knew why I had "felt" she needed a male dog. Suddenly, I knew why she and Spartacus were destined to be together. They would fill a void in each other's lives. They would take care of each other. He would be the strong male presence that she lacks. And she, a gentle, feminine presence for him.

And so it was that on Valentine's Day in 2009, Spartacus found the love of his life. And experienced the true power of an open heart.

It was no accident that Spartacus came to me after I was further along in my own healing process. Had the timing been different, I might not have been able to help him. But because I had been assisted with healing, I could in turn help him. Such is the order and the way of the universe—which bestows immeasurable gifts that in turn must be shared with the greater whole of humanity so that the beauty in the lesson may be recycled over and over again.

Valiant

"What else do we know about him?" I asked.

"I'm pretty sure he was beaten," Sandy answered.

"Really? I asked him that when I went into him. He said that it wasn't that bad."

"That's what abused children say too."

Sandy was right. Valiant was abused. I won't go into the details. It's not the point of his story. The point is that abuse is abuse. There is no tolerable amount. There is no point at which it is okay. And there is no sliding scale to mediate what is acceptable. Abuse is abuse. And Valiant was terrified of everything as a result of what he'd been through.

His new name would embody a bold, new start and infuse him with a sense of courage he had long since lost. We hoped that he could become as brave and bold as his name implied.

When I saw his photo for the first time, I sensed he had a prey drive. I thought I could see it in his eyes. When I met him in person, I saw that his prey drive, along with pretty much everything else, had been pounded out of him.

My daughter and I met him at an adoption event, thinking we might foster him and help him recover. But he was tough to handle, and his primary focus was to escape. He strained against his leash, and his claws scratched at the concrete sidewalk. A panic of paws scrambling in every direction.

I implored his handler to give me some time alone with him. But the handler didn't know me and didn't think I could manage him. Caron stepped in and assured him I would be fine. And I took Valiant aside.

"Honey, relax. You've nothing to fear here."

No response.

"How can I help you?"

Why am I here?

"To find a new home. A good home. With new people."

This is impossible.

"Why?"

I don't fit in.

"Why?"

I'm not good enough.

"Who told you that?"

My last people.

"What happened?"

Nothing I ever did was good enough for them.

"So you were abused then?"

I told you. It wasn't that bad.

"That is in the past. You are safe. No one will ever harm you again."

No response.

He relaxed a little, but his trust would not be won overnight.

Since we had three acres of unfenced property in the country and Valiant seemed intent on running away, it was decided that we were probably not the right home for him at this point. Instead, Coastal placed him with two of their longtime volunteers.

I'd brought some Bach flower essences for him—homeopathic drops developed by British physician Dr. Edward Bach. Dr. Bach saw disease as an end product; a final stage; a physical manifestation of unhappiness, fear, and worry. So he looked to nature to find healing flowers that assist in overcoming challenges.

I purchased blends specifically for Valiant—Mimulus for fear and Vervain for courage. I gave these to his new fosters with instructions about how to administer them.

His fosters worked their magic with him. Week by week, he gained confidence and lost fear. By his third adoption event, he was a different dog, greeting people with shy restraint instead of gripping fear. And he went home with a loving family that would continue to nurture his healing process.

I tuned into him a few days after his adoption and asked him how he was. He told me that his new people were kind and that their love was beginning to eclipse the fear that used to reside in his heart. He said he was truly happy now and he no longer feared the human touch. Valiant is a shining example of the innocent reception and the forgiving nature of the animal kingdom. They do not judge, and most retain their ability to love and trust—even after experiencing the worst from humans.

It is said that there are no accidents in life. If that is true, perhaps Valiant is a reminder that we come in with a plan, a blueprint by which we chart and navigate through our life journey. And even if that life is harsh or painful, there are lessons to be learned there. And perhaps Valiant's purpose was to allow his people a chance to rise above old patterns of abuse and power. Instead, he fell victim to unfortunate circumstances that were beyond his power to change.

And even though his life was marred by abuse, we are eternally grateful that Valiant found his way to Coastal and that his journey ended with the beautiful gifts of love and courage.

Giada

A thin black and tan shepherd jogged down the dirt trail cut into the side of the hill and circled the lawn, sniffing just outside my office window at work. My phone rang. The shepherd jogged off in search of something I couldn't see.

"Did you see that?" It was Stefanie, one of my teammates in the marketing department. Her office was directly above mine, one floor up. "A German shepherd just came down the trail. I had to call you. You've been looking for a German shepherd. Maybe this is the one. Maybe it's coming to find you."

"I did see. I should go. It might be lost."

I walked down the hall and out the back door of the office building. Two colleagues had gathered, watching the dog scale the steep dirt bank beyond the parking lot and paw furiously at a gopher hole. Two more colleagues joined to watch.

I approached. The energy felt female. So I assumed it was a girl.

"Hi, beauty. Are you lost?"

No response.

"Will you come to me? I won't hurt you."

No response.

But she stared at me in disbelief. She'd never had someone talk to her.

"Be careful, Dobie," Ricardo called out after me. "German shepherds are vicious."

I smiled. I knew I wasn't in danger. She meant me no harm. Nor I her.

I picked my way up the first few feet of the steep bank. She watched me come and returned to her digging. I stopped a few feet downhill from her.

"Can you come to me?"

I could tell that she understood me. She was curious that I was talking to her. But she was intent on capturing whatever was down in the hole, and she turned and dug voraciously.

She was a classic black and tan, and despite being rail thin, surprisingly, her soft luxuriant coat was in beautiful shape. Her distinctive and pronounced nose was now caked with dirt from her quest for squirrel.

For ten minutes, I coaxed her unsuccessfully. I changed tactics and walked down the bank to get food. A colleague dug through her lunch box and offered some leftover turkey.

I approached her, turkey in hand, and tossed a piece to her. She took a step toward me and retrieved the meat. I stepped back and tossed another piece. She stepped forward and gulped the turkey. One more piece and she was mine. A pink and silver collar and tags hung from her neck. I fingered the tag and read her name. Giada. She had belonged to someone at some point. But I suspected she'd been a stray for at least a couple of months. This poor girl was thin as a rail but beautiful despite lack of food. I slipped two fingers under her collar and led her off the hill, then knelt to feed her the last piece of turkey from my hand. She gulped it gratefully licking the residue from my fingers.

I handed her to a colleague and asked her to hold the dog while I ran back to my office to retrieve my cell phone. Unfortunately, I returned without my glasses. I couldn't read the number on the tag. Luckily, my colleague wasn't also losing her eyesight. She read the number to me, and I punched it into my cell. It rang once, and a man answered.

"Hello?"

"Are you missing a German shepherd?"

"Yes! You have her?"

"Yes. Has she been missing long?"

"Just ten minutes."

His response shocked me. She wasn't a stray? She wasn't lost? She looked like she'd been foraging for food for weeks.

We exchanged information, and I walked her to the front entrance of our office parking lot. I stopped at our company sign and saw the dog's owner already walking up the long hill to our offices. She recognized him without emotion. No relief, no joy. Nothing. She simply watched him walk up the hill. I thought it was odd that she wasn't happy to see him. But I let it go. She wasn't lost or homeless or scared. She was just exploring.

He took her by the collar and shook his head ruefully. "I thought I'd give her some space and she takes off." He wasn't thrilled.

I looked at him for a moment and sized him up. A thin man in his late thirties. He wore jeans and a T-shirt promoting some band I didn't know. Wild, frizzy red hair restrained in a ponytail and a matching beard made him look like a modern-day member of ZZ Top.

He turned away. As he did, I took a deep breath and plunged. "I'm not trying to be judgmental, but your dog needs to gain twenty pounds."

"What?"

"Your dog...she needs to gain weight. I work with a German shepherd rescue. She's far thinner than any of our dogs."

"Oh, she's not a purebred German shepherd."

I stared at him in disbelief and repeated myself in staccato, punching every word and hoping to hammer it home.

"Your...dog...needs...to...gain...twenty...pounds." I stared directly into his eyes.

He shrugged, then nodded and walked away. I wondered if I'd done the right thing. What had I just sent her back to? If he was so clueless that he didn't know she was drastically underweight, what else was he neglecting? Was he more than neglectful? Did he abuse her too? Would it have been appropriate for me to intervene further without any proof?

I had his phone number. I could call animal control. I could ask them to follow up. Not to be punitive. But to educate him.

I "went" to Giada a few days later.

"Are you getting enough food?"

You got through to him.

"Is he ever abusive?"

Impatient, not abusive.

"Do you like him?"

He'll do.

"I'm sorry you don't have someone as evolved as you in your life."

Next time.

I retreated from the conversation and pondered her words and the purpose of her relationship with this man. Why are so many people clueless to the needs of their animal companions? I closed my eyes and asked for guidance. A voice whispered quietly in the recesses of my head.

When the pupil is ready to learn, the teacher will appear.

There was truth in the statement, and I know this because I've experienced it myself. Whenever I am ready to move beyond the status quo, learn a new skill, or take on something new, there is always someone who steps in to help me with that phase in my journey.

Each of us is, at some point in time, ignorant. Ignorant to a lesson we are here to learn. Ignorant to a way of being we have not yet grown into. But when we are ready to learn and grow and stretch, the teacher appears.

Giada is this man's teacher. She has been put in his life to assist with his expansion, to teach him to balance the masculine authority figure with the feminine nurturer in order to understand what a true caretaker looks like. She is here to help him grow. And if he is open to her wisdom, he will benefit immensely.

Patience and Eve

We called them "pocket shepherds" because they're pint-sized and could practically fit in your pocket. It was the perfect description for Patience and Eve, two dogs on separate but parallel paths whose lives merged when they met at Coastal German Shepherd Rescue.

Like many of the dogs we meet, Patience had been found as a stray, living on the streets, trying to care for herself and ten puppies. Not an easy task for a malnourished mother. In one sense, being picked up and placed in the dog shelter was a saving grace; in another, it could have been a death sentence. In the shelter, she was fed and cared for, but even with food and care, she struggled to mother her litter of ten. And in a high-kill shelter, life is a waiting game where days are numbered.

She waited patiently and hoped for help to come along. And one day it seemed that her dreams had come true. That hope had arrived. She waited again, watching patiently as her rescuers lifted each puppy, barely four weeks old, one by one, out of her cage. Dutiful mother that she was, she waited to be lifted out as well. But as the last puppy was removed, the kennel door was closed in her face. And the organization that had come and taken her puppies left Patience behind.

Now Patience found herself on death row, alone in a cold, scary concrete cell, on a list to be euthanized. Her fate seemed certain until someone intervened. Someone with a heart of gold who wanted Patience, still a puppy herself, to have a brighter future.

Coastal was contacted and came to her rescue the next day. But this poor girl was so afraid, she didn't want to leave her cage. And who could blame her after what she'd been through? Finally, her rescuers from Coastal coaxed this fearful pup from the back of the kennel, and with each step, Patience came closer to freedom.

But she was traumatized by her experiences with humans. She cowered around people even though they meant her no harm. Her only comfort seemed to be the presence of other dogs. But over time, she began to open up. She gained confidence by watching us handle the other dogs. She learned that human touch can be good, and not everyone will hurt or abandon her.

When I met her at Coastal's kennels, she tenderly licked my hand and won my heart with her gentle soul.

In part two of this story, we meet Eve, a petite female. Like Patience, Eve was young, pretty, shy, and unassuming. Like Patience, Eve was an abandoned mother who had recently birthed a litter of six. The only difference was that Eve got to keep her puppies until they were ready to be weaned. She got to see them placed in loving homes as she patiently waited her turn for a forever home.

Patience and Eve bunked together in Coastal's kennels, becoming fast friends and connecting deeply. At adoption events, the two girls were inseparable, lying nose to nose in their crate, walking side by side, even meeting new people together. They drew strength from each another. Over time, we began to fear that if we had to place them in separate homes, these two dear dogs would suffer yet another loss. We prayed that they would be adopted together.

But they were often overlooked at the adoption events. They didn't fit most people's list of criteria. They lacked the classic, regal look that stamps most of the shepherd breed. They were small. They had droopy ears. And they were just so sad.

One day, a couple at one of Coastal's adoption events was interested in Patience. After spending almost two hours with the two girls, they were so touched by the deep bond between Patience and Eve that they too couldn't bear to separate them. Especially after they'd endured so much heartache. At the end of the day, the couple announced that they'd adopt both so that Patience and Eve could live out their lives together.

We were thrilled and offered to cut the usual adoption fee in half. But this kind, beautiful couple donated more than Coastal asked for so that funds could go to save other dogs. It was one of the most heartwarming things I've seen.

I never tried to identify what Patience and Eve were here to teach us. Nor did I ask them. Was it that if you have patience your dreams will come true? Was it that on the eve where things seem darkest morning comes anew, ripe with promise? Was it that you must not let the disappointments of the past keep you from forming heartfelt connections in the future? Or was it simply a testimony to the power of friendship and its ability to heal us and lift us up when all seems lost?

Whatever it was, Patience and Eve touched our hearts. We will always remember how these two—glued at the hip, side by side, nose to nose—drew strength and courage from each other. And led each other out of the dark and into a bright new future.

Maggie

I debated long and hard about including Maggie's story. The cruelty and abuse she endured is difficult to process and even harder to fathom. But her story and her message are far too important to omit. So I share it with the forewarning that the first two pages contains graphic content.

When our volunteers found Maggie at the shelter, she lay limp like a rag doll, her coat caked in feces and urine. Unable to walk or remove herself from her own waste, she barely had the strength to lift her head to eat. And a miscommunication at the shelter meant that the minimal pain medication she was supposed to receive hadn't been administered for the last twelve hours. When she saw Jess, she lifted her beautiful head and fixed her with sad brown eyes that revealed a courage and strength that masked her pain.

Jess wrapped her in a blanket, lifted her gingerly, carried her into a crate lined with a soft pillow and blankets, and drove straight to the hospital. Maggie was cleaned, hydrated, and given IV pain medication.

X-rays revealed that Maggie had a broken pelvis. This would be nothing compared to the full horror Maggie had experienced. Maggie came to us burdened with a two-pound chain hanging from her neck and riddled with entry wounds from a BB gun. The vet's diagnosis was that Maggie might have been chained and used for target practice, and when she could endure no more, she escaped somehow, dragging part of the chain with her, only to be hit by a car and taken to a high-kill shelter where she lay helpless for days.

It reminded me of the disgusting practice called a "canned hunt" in which human predators armed with guns and jeeps stalk and kill animals held captive in small fenced enclosures. All in the name of sport so a human can claim a trophy.

Maggie's story was shared with a few core volunteers via email. When I read it, I went numb and then curled in a ball and sobbed. Waves of nausea wracked my body. I raced to the bathroom and threw up.

I try to look at the world from a place of compassion. I try not to compartmentalize into good or bad but rather appropriate and inappropriate. I try not to judge or point fingers because perhaps I'm not privy to the big picture or all the facts. I try to tell myself that everything happens for a reason. But I am not at the point in my expansion or evolution where I can apply any of these statements to Maggie's plight. And I never will be.

What happened to Maggie was not merely inappropriate. It was wrong. The people who did this to her are cruel beyond imagination. And while it is better to forgive and forget, it is my fervent wish that the people responsible will be caught and locked away in a cell inhabited by some hardened criminal with a devout love of animals and full knowledge of what happened to Maggie. That would be justice.

Maggie faced a daunting surgery, performed in steps to minimize the risk. The first step would be to move her hips back into place and secure them with pins and screws. Another step would require the amputation of her entire tail. For the time being, the BB gun pellets would have to remain where they were.

You may wonder why we would go to such extreme measures to save one life. Quite simply because we will have made a difference. In Maggie's case, she will feel the gentle touch of a loving hand and the tears of someone who cares. And even if she didn't survive, she would know that she mattered and she would leave this world embraced in love and dignity and honor.

Maggie underwent the first surgery to stabilize the two fractures in her pelvic region. Her hip joint was secured with pins and screws. A large hematoma in her back leg was lanced, drained, and wrapped to ease the swelling. The fracture at the base of her tail was realigned but much of it would still need to be amputated.

Then the healing waiting game began.

Maggie came through the surgery like a champ. She was in good spirits and won over the hospital staff with her happy demeanor and loving nature. She was a model patient, allowing the staff to handle and treat her, never once snapping or snarling.

The doctors ordered full bed rest so that her bones and especially the tail fracture would knit. Her hospital stay was extended to ensure full-time supervised care. In time, she was released to the care of a loving foster.

But Maggie's healing process was just beginning. No medical procedures existed to heal her trust and her broken heart. During the first week in her foster home, she cowered at the slightest touch and sought constant refuge in her crate. Slowly, gently her foster won her trust. Maggie began to feel safe and secure and eventually began to enjoy attention and affection, seeking the loving hands of the people she lived with.

Maggie's stitches healed, and she began pool therapy to strengthen her muscles and stimulate circulation in the hopes that it would speed the healing process and break down scar tissue. But it was still too early to finalize a diagnosis in regard to her nerves and incontinence issues. Once Maggie began to walk, we discovered yet another blow for our brave girl. Her foster noticed the injury when Maggie developed a decided limp in her front leg. X-rays revealed that Maggie's left shoulder was dislocated from the socket due to a shattered scapula. This meant additional surgery to restore the use of her front leg and months of physical therapy.

I went to Maggie after her surgery.

"Maggie. Have no fear. The people in your life will never harm you. They only want what is best for you."

Thank you.

"Can you trust again?"

I think that is clear.

"Does that mean yes or no?"

I will.

"Were you with those horrible people long?"

About a year.

I had to withdraw. Tears streamed down my face. My throat knotted tight and ached. I waited. Then composed myself and went back in.

"I'm so sorry. It kills me that you endured this."

None of us endures anything alone.

Her noble words overwhelmed me. I withdrew again. Sobbing. My chest heaved, and my throat ached. I steeled myself again and went back in.

"Is there anything you need?"

I want for nothing.

"Do you know that you are loved?"

It has been clear since that kind woman removed me from my cage.

"You mean when you were in the shelter?"

If you mean the dirty place with the cold hard floor, then yes.

"Is there anything else you want me to know?"

I am alive, and I have a second chance.

Tears welled again and stung my eyes. But this time I stayed with her.

"What are your hopes now?"

To live a great life.

"I promise we will make that happen."

As I withdrew, I pondered the power in her message.

None of us endures anything alone.

It's true. None of us goes it alone. Guidance, assistance, and support come in many forms. How often do we ignore this or fail to reach out and ask for what we need, all in the name of pride?

I gave thought to what coming to Coastal might have meant for Maggie. It's far more than just being free from abuse. As she indicated, it is the beginning of a new life and a time of rebirth. Like winter yielding to spring, the promise of hope, unity, and abundance surge forth, revealing the ultimate potential of a new day.

Unfortunately, abuse is common in the animal kingdom. And we are all responsible. Responsible for being aware, responsible for speaking up when we see it, and responsible for playing the role of change agent. If each of us were to shoulder just one piece of this responsibility, we would make a difference and perhaps obliterate abuse from our world. Completely.

Maggie was adopted by her foster family. They couldn't bear to have her start over anywhere else. They coaxed her from a terrified, emaciated, broken soul to a beautiful, loving, and thriving girl. Now she tumbles and wrestles with her canine family. Now the fears of the past have been erased. She is a new dog. And she now has just what she wished for—the chance to live a great life.

Hanson

Every week, there is a new one. A handsome male who reminds me of Blitz: stout, alpha, masculine, regal, with a sweet and loving heart…and a prey drive. And every week, I fall in love. It was becoming an inside joke at Coastal. If it was a male and I fell for him, it was almost guaranteed the boy would be bad with cats.

His name was Hanson. But we nicknamed him Handsome, because he was. Hanson was medium height, built sturdy and square. Red and black and tan with an unusual blue-grey dusting at the tips of the black in his fur. Dramatic, pale golden eyes fixed you with a direct stare, one that implied intelligence and curiosity, as compared to the commanding energy of Klaus.

I watched Rob, an experienced volunteer and dog trainer, walk Hanson at his first event. A few paces behind, I handled another dog. It was early morning, just before the adoption event. All the dogs are amped before the event. The cool ocean air. The chaos of twenty plus dogs—some friends, some strangers—

going through their paces. And the excitement of the twenty-minute ride to PetSmart. All combine to make most dogs a little hard to handle at first.

But clearly Hanson hadn't spent much time on a leash. He reared and backflipped to avoid the collar. When that didn't work, he jumped on Rob repeatedly. Rob ducked and turned his back to avoid Hanson's attempts to jump him. And continued to work patiently to redirect him.

All we knew about him was that his owner had died, leaving his and his sister's fate in the air. They'd been willed to the man's daughter. But she knew nothing about handling big dogs. Let alone smart ones. Shepherds are happy to toe the line…once you prove you're alpha. You have to earn their respect and the right to that respect. The woman didn't know how to go about this. She was intimidated by Hanson's size and the "reputation" shepherds have. So she'd contacted Coastal to relinquish the pair.

Later that day, a volunteer handed him to me to walk so he could get another dog out of its crate to show a prospective owner. I took him outside. His gait was light and springy. He turned and jumped on me. I turned my back. He did it again. I pushed him off and asked him to sit. He lowered his haunches slowly, reluctantly. I praised him and bent to put my arm around his shoulders. And I told him not to be afraid, that we would find him a good home. He looked at me in confusion. He didn't understand how I could be talking to him. All dogs are confused or surprised at first, then delighted.

Within five minutes, he walked calmly by my side as if he'd just graduated from obedience school.

"You did a good job with him," I commented, walking past Rob. "It's like he's been walking on a leash for years."

Hanson and I bonded quickly. Each time I'd stop and bend to hug him, he lavished me with kisses. But now, my heart didn't twist when the dogs showed me affection. There was no sadness attached to the fact that it wasn't Blitz. It was simply loving and joyful. And I adored this sweet, sweet boy back. A couple of the volunteers teased me about falling for him because of his obvious prey drive. I did know how to pick them, I thought, and I smiled ruefully.

Why don't you take me? he asked.

"Honey, you'd be mine in a heartbeat. But I can tell you wouldn't be good with cats."

No. I think I failed my cat test.

"That's what I heard."

Later that day, we sought refuge from the heat in the cool, cave-like store interior. I sank to the floor, and Hanson stretched out next to me. He placed his paws and forearms gently over my legs. Partly to connect, partly to protect. I was becoming *his* human.

Suddenly, I saw my dear friend Jill, who had first taught me to communicate with animals. She stood with her husband on the other side of our event space, across a slew of Coastal's volunteers and other dogs. I jumped to my feet and pointed to a space away from the other dogs. And we joined up, hugging warmly.

"Check out my new love," I said, beaming proudly at Hanson.

"He's gorgeous," Jill agreed. "This dog is super smart, Dobie. Highly intelligent."

"He is," I nodded. "This is his first day on a leash, we think, and he's practically perfect."

We chatted for a while, and Jill and her husband continued to admire Hanson. They left reluctantly, casting an admiring glance at all our beautiful shepherds.

At the end of the day, Hanson had not been adopted, so I loaded him into his transport van and told him his time would come.

At the adoption event the following week, my morning was consumed by handling another dog. But I felt Hanson's eyes on me the whole time. Watching. Waiting. Finally, I switched dogs and took Hanson out of his crate. He was overjoyed to see me and I him. I walked him until the event wound down.

We began to pack things up, and I held Hanson until his transport was ready. Dogs were brought out of their crates and stood at attention, waiting their turn to leave. The noise and activity started getting to Hanson. His nerves were frayed from the long day. He started barking. I bent and put my arm around him but couldn't calm him. I took him outside to wait by the transport van, away from the din and noise of the event. We relaxed on the grass, and he lay under my bent legs. We didn't speak. We didn't need to. Hanson was so smart. He seemed to know exactly what was happening at any moment.

One of our volunteers jogged toward me. Someone at the event wanted to see Hanson. We returned to PetSmart and connected with the prospective owner. I ushered him out to the parking lot, and we took Hanson for a walk. The guy seemed nice, intelligent, and caring. He grilled me about Hanson. I grilled him back. But it was late in the day, and he was unsure about making a commitment.

"You could foster to adopt," I offered.

"What does that mean?"

"It means you fill out all the paperwork and take him, and if in a week it doesn't work out, you can bring him back."

This appealed to him. The truth is that Coastal will take any dog back at any time, no questions asked. Their main concern is for the dog and its wellbeing.

I led him back to the adoption event, where we concluded the paperwork. I stayed with him, savoring my last few moments with Hanson. The man commented a couple of times about how attached Hanson seemed to be to me, but I told him that in a couple of days Hanson would be just as attached to him. That's just the way he is. And yet, I felt our bond had been special.

It's a touch bittersweet when dogs you love get adopted. You're thrilled for them of course—that's the whole point. To give them a fresh start in a forever home. But you know that most likely you'll never see them again. And that the next few events will feel a bit empty in comparison.

Hanson now lives happily ever after with the man who fostered him. He tells me that he is loved and contented. There is much to do in his new home, and he has a teenage boy to play with. Exactly what he was longing for.

Hanson, like many of Coastal's dogs allowed me to relive the connection I had with Blitz. Warm, beautiful, and heartfelt. He reminds us to be thankful for simple pleasures, to appreciate life's special moments, and to treasure our friendships because it is these things that make life worth living. Hanson was a gift that I treasured. And he will remain that way forever.

Baghera

When our kitty Tigger passed away, Blitz was still with us, so I resisted getting another cat for months. Because he'd never been great with her. But my son wanted kittens, and he waged a vigilant campaign. One day he called me from work.

"Mom, I'm at the feed store. What would you think if I brought two kittens home?"

"You know what I'd think."

"But you should see them, Mom. And they'd give them to us for free if we bought a bag of cat food."

"Hardly an incentive. Free kittens are a dime a dozen."

"Come on, Mom."

I sighed. "What colors?"

"One's black with a little white spot. The other's a cute tiger."

"I don't know."

"Please?"

"Caden, I really think that Blitz doesn't want to have to live with kittens."

"Okay." He hung up dejectedly.

A wave of sadness washed over me. And then the realization that somehow we'd been connected to these kittens before. That they were meant to be with us.

I dialed Caden's cell phone.

"Okay. Go get them."

We named the tiger Taz. Short for Tasmanian Devil. And the black one, Baghera. Reminiscent of *The Jungle Book*'s panther. We called him Baggie for short. Baghera was personality plus. My daughter observed one day that had he been human, he might have been a nudist. His trademark move was to loll lazily on his back, limbs spread-eagle, meowing for someone to come rub his belly. And he had the most distinctive meow. Like a long, drawn-out southern drawl.

At first, they were so small they fit easily into the palm of my hand. And for weeks they were tiny enough to fit into a lap at the same time. Often they'd fight while lying together in my lap. It was the cutest thing.

One morning I rose sleepily and walked into the kitchen for water. As I stood in front of the sink, they jumped me from behind and their weight pulled my pajama pants to my ankles, leaving me nude from the waist down. I laughed so hard I almost lost my balance.

I'd never seen two cats that were more connected. Taz and Baggie were inseparable. Almost glued at the hip.

They'd curl up and groom each other and sleep with their arms around each other. It was like they were lovers. It was almost odd to me that two boys would seem to share such a deep and heartfelt connection.

They grew fast, and soon both were fourteen inches in length. And once they were bigger, I began to let them outside for an hour each morning. But I'd trained them to come back when I called. Thanks to Feline Greenies. They were crazy for them. All I had to do was go outside and call and shake the bag and they'd scamper headlong toward the back door.

One morning, I let them out for a romp. An hour later, I called them in. Taz jogged casually up the back stairs and along the sidewalk to the patio. No sign of Baghera. I shrugged and let Taz inside. Baghera would be back before the kids left for their classes. They could let him back in the house when they woke.

That night I returned from work and let myself into the house. The kids were in the family room doing homework. I walked in to greet them.

"Baghera didn't come back," Hailey said. It felt like an accusation.

"What! Did you look for him?"

"Yes. Three times. I looked everywhere."

A knot formed in the pit of my stomach. I grabbed a flashlight and walked numbly around my property and up and down the driveway and adjacent roads. I kept calling his name and trilling "kitty kitty kitty" over and over.

At ten o'clock, I reluctantly gave up and came into the house to comfort Taz. He was distraught and wandered the house and the halls uttering pitiful, painful meows.

I took him in my arms and tried to comfort him. I started to cry. I could feel his sorrow. I carried him into my room and sunk into bed with him in my arms, and we stayed that way for hours until he got up and left.

The next day, I worked from home. I still couldn't believe that Baghera was gone. I planned to look again as soon as it was light enough. Taz was desperate to go out. Though I was fearful, I felt I had to let him go. He needed to look for his brother. I couldn't let my fear keep him prisoner. I held the sliding glass door open, and he looked back at me, over his shoulder. I hoped he wasn't saying goodbye. He slipped through the open door and was swallowed by the early morning darkness. I truly felt I might never see him again. I broke down and wept.

Darkness gave way to grey, overcast clouds. I worked at the computer in the family room in front of a window that overlooked a huge rock outcropping. Something caught my eye, and I quickly turned. Two coyotes strolled casually through my backyard like they were domesticated dogs. One stopped and looked through the sliding glass door. The other joined him and then took off as I stood. The straggler stared directly into my eyes. Are you kidding me? I thought. He showed no fear.

I walked out to shoo him away. In the back of my head, a voice whispered that it might not be a good idea to confront a wild animal that wasn't exhibiting any fear. And yet I kept walking, aware that I wasn't carrying a weapon. As I approached, it took flight. Down my dirt drive and up a plateau, where it stopped and turned to look at me again.

"Did you take my cat?" I was numb.

I was the one.

Our eyes locked. I knew this was symbolic, but I didn't know why. It was a strange connection. Perhaps he was just surprised that we were communicating. After a moment, he jogged off, and several others joined him from their hiding places in the brush. It was a wakeup call. The wilderness had merged with the civilized world. The line separating our two worlds had become blurred and would only become more so as more land was developed and their territory shrank. I had been naïve and blind to the shift and ignorant in thinking that because I only let Taz and Baghera out for an hour or so, that alone would keep them safe.

I turned back and went in the house. Taz emerged on the back patio. Oh my God, I thought, he'd been right behind the coyotes. I scooped him up and brought him in. I never let him outside again. But I continued to look for Baghera for days. It felt to me that he was still around. Maybe hiding or maybe in a neighbor's home.

I spent extra time with Taz, trying to ease his grief. One night as I held him, he felt different. It seemed that his grief had been replaced with a sense of peace. But there was more. It was almost as though Baghera's spirit had entered him. As though for now at least they had integrated and become one.

I kept expecting Baghera to show up. But he didn't. Finally, after four days, I had to admit that Baghera was indeed gone. We each grieved in our own way. And after a few weeks, we decided that Taz needed a feline companion. We simply weren't enough for him.

My daughter and I went to the Humane Society to look. Two cats caught our attention. One a dramatic rust-orange tabby. But she was aloof, and we sensed she wasn't a match for Taz.

The other, an adorable, silky female the color of brushed nickel. Her steel-hued fur gave the appearance of a silver outline at the ends. She was so petite her front legs were the width of my index fingers. We opened her cage, and she butted my hands with her head, shrugging and arching her body against my hands and shoulders. She chewed softly on my fingertips, purring like a tiny, joyful buzz saw. She won us over with her charm, and we adopted Kanga on the spot.

When we brought her home, she hid for two days. Later, she'd emerge briefly and dart about the room like a little ferret. On day three, there was a lot of hissing and growling as she and Taz established their relationship. On day four, Kanga became a little flirt. She'd roll on her back and flip back and forth, front paws outstretched to get Taz's attention, and approach him with her back arched coyly to groom him and butt up against him. She was hard to resist. After two more days, he gave in and started grooming her back. Soon they were fast friends. Running, play-fighting in a roly-poly ball of flipping fur and tails. And sleeping together, curled as one, just like Taz used to do with Baggie.

Dr. Edward Bach, who dedicated his life to researching and perfecting the system of flower essence healing, has a belief about healing energy. That it raises our inner nature and brings us nearer to our souls and, by that very act, brings us peace and relieves our sufferings. Like a beautiful painting or an uplifting song or a glorious sunset. We can be inspired and healed by that which surrounds us.

Little Kanga, beautiful and uplifting and glorious, helped each of us heal from the loss of Baghera. And while he will never be replaced, the void that he left was eventually filled with a different kind of feline energy.

Fozzy

Jim Henson must have had this guy in mind when he
created the character of Fozzie Bear. Part teddy bear,
part sheep, our Fozzy was a German shepherd-Great
Pyrenees cross with soft ears and paws the size of
clenched fists. Stout-limbed, his forelegs were as thick
as my upper arms. He was wide-backed like an airport
runway—you could have landed a plane on him. He
was by far the biggest dog we'd fostered. His coat was
downy and llama-like, and he shed in pillowy clumps.

It was early spring, but a freak Santa Ana wind hit,
blowing dry, hot air through Southern California.
Coastal's kennels were full, and we were trying to save
six additional dogs from death row. A frantic email
went out, requesting more foster homes. My daughter
and I read the short bios for each of the six dogs in
need. And since his bio stated that Fozzy was good with
cats, we decided that he should come live with us.

His first evening with us, Fozzy was understandably
conflicted. He didn't know whether to bond with all of
us or none of us. Was he staying, or were we simply

another pit stop? Should he connect with me, the alpha female in the home; with my son, the most fun and playful; or with my daughter, arguably the most seasoned trainer in the house? In his first few hours, he wandered our home from person to person, unable to settle. Finally, he crashed from sheer exhaustion.

I'm not sure I would describe Fozzy as "good with cats." At first, he was just interested in them. He seemed to want to play with them. Then he became more interested, chasing in earnest. Taz tried to stand his ground, but Fozzy's need to play overshadowed his caution about Taz's claws. Nothing seemed to faze this guy. But he was good about backing off at a firm "no."

At just under a year, Fozzy was still a puppy. With lots of cute puppy antics. He was mouthy. He liked to carry articles of clothing around in his teeth. He seemed to be especially intrigued with my lingerie. If I left laundry around, I'd find lace bras and camisoles and other items of underwear strewn casually around the house. One day I replaced a pair of soft black socks in their drawer at least five times while Fozzy "helped" me tidy up.

Fozzy ran the gamut between low-key and frenetic. Most of the day, he was happy to chill at your feet. But when the mood struck, he'd race around like a greyhound running laps. It was funny when he was outside. Not quite as funny when he turned the living room into a racetrack and crashed into a cabinet where I store my collectible dishes. The bull in the china shop had nothing on Fozzy.

About two or three times a day, he'd turn into a Tasmanian Devil, a tour de force of fur pounding the ground as he galloped gaily around our property. After five or ten minutes, he'd be done and downshift into neutral again. But without the opportunity to blow off steam, Fozzy would have been a handful.

The first time I talked to him, I was working at the kitchen table, pounding away on my laptop. I looked down at him as he lay by my feet. He stared deeply into my eyes.

"What?" I asked.

I like it here.

"Better than the kennels?"

Yeah.

"What happened to your people?"

They dropped me off.

"Why?"

I got too big. Their house was small.

"So they left you."

High and dry.

"It happens a lot. People don't know what they're getting into when they get a small puppy. They get wrapped up in the moment, and they don't see that down the road a puppy will get big. It's not your fault."

I know.

"But you'd think that, even when you were little, one look at your paws should have given them a clue."

You'd think.

"You're a smart boy."

I am.

"How much exercise did you used to get in your last home?"

Hardly any.

Then he lay down on his side with a heavy thump and slept. But now I had my answer, and I knew why he'd been relinquished. The people probably had an apartment. They hardly ever walked him or did anything with him. They didn't know how to handle his energy spurts.

As I came to know Fozzy better, it occurred to me that he was the class clown— the comic relief in a sea of Coastal's dogs. Most of whom come to us reeling from a past of abuse, or neglect, or ignorance.

Not Fozzy. He refused to let his past experience keep him from finding joy in the simple things, from loving openly, and from trusting again. He seemed unfazed by being dumped in a high-kill shelter. He wasn't scared, or sad, or distrusting. He was simply happy. He even panted with a silly grin.

Everything was a game to him. Everything a new adventure or mystery to be explored. He was a master at amusing himself. He'd toss a ball in the air and pounce on it. Or strew magazines haphazardly around on the carpet and then dash from a distance to skate on them like a kid on a skim board at the beach. Or his trademark move: flying off the bank in my backyard, paws outstretched a la Superman. All he lacked was a cape.

Mark Twain has belief about the power of humor. That it is a great and saving thing. That in the presence of humor our irritations and resentments slip away, and a sunny spirit takes their place. This was certainly true in Fozzy's case.

As time passed, he became better with the cats. With Taz at least. Kanga mostly hid under my bed. One day, Taz slept soundly on the corner of my bed. Fozzy and I were picking up things he'd dragged out. He wandered casually over to my bed and licked Taz on the head. Taz woke up and sleepily allowed Fozzy to continue to lick him. I watched cautiously. Spartacus had done that too, and the next thing I knew, he had Baghera by the head. Fozzy poked at Taz with his nose, coaxing him to run. Then eased two front paws gingerly on the bed and stood semi-erect.

"Fozzy!"

His head snapped toward me, and he plunked his feet back on the floor and jogged casually toward me, panting happily. Then he flopped obediently on the floor and watched me fold socks.

We fell in love with Fozzy from the moment he came to stay with us. My children begged to keep him. But I sensed we weren't the best home for Fozzy. We weren't a bad home, but we weren't the best. We lived inland on three brushy acres. Summers are hot, and his thick, plush coat would have made him miserable. Plus, he was a magnet for burrs and foxtails. I spent hours picking stuff out of his fur.

I felt that he needed a home with kids and other dogs to play with. A home where he wouldn't need to make up his own games when the urge to play hit and we were busy. And as much as we loved him, I felt we owed it to him to find the best home, knowing if he was meant to be with us, nothing would materialize.

I asked him one day what kind of home he wanted.

How about you?

"Oh, honey. You need a home with kids and other dogs."

Why?

"Because you're a puppy, and you need to play."

I play here.

"Yes, but wouldn't you like to have kids and dogs to play games and romp with? Doesn't that sound like fun?"

Fun. Fun. Fun.

"You *are* a comedian."

Although Fozzy was a clown, he was also highly intelligent. I sensed it the first time I looked into his eyes. And he proved my instincts right with his ability to learn commands quickly. But it was more than that. He seemed to know how to read people. One morning, I lay on the floor to do sit-ups. I figured Fozzy would interpret this as an invitation to play and attack me while I was vulnerable. But instead, he gently licked my face. When I didn't respond, he understood that I wanted him to stop. Then he lay down by my side and licked my hand gently until I got up.

We'd only had Fozzy five days when I received an email from Coastal's leader that someone was interested in him. They'd been visiting our website every day for a month, looking for a big fuzzy male. As I read the message, I couldn't believe my eyes. The interested family had two female dogs. They lived by the coast, with a huge fenced yard. It sounded like the perfect home. I almost cried from sheer delight.

Two days later, I took Fozzy for the meet-and-greet and did a home inspection. The family fell in love with him and adopted him on the spot. It was everything I dreamed for him. A young dog to play with, a huge fenced yard, daily walks in a private fenced park. The husband worked from home, and the wife even made organic dog food from scratch! It was truly perfection.

Fozzy's new family sends me updates from time to time. He integrated beautifully, and they adore him. They thanked us profusely for bringing Fozzy into their lives.

Quite often, when I meet our dogs, I wonder how their previous people could have let them go. How could they just abandon them or turn them into a shelter? It's like discarding a member of the family. Especially a dog like Fozzy, who was so joyful, beautiful, and eager to please.

What I came to realize was that like all relationships, some are meant to last forever and others are not. Some of us search for years to find the person with whom we are meant to be. Some of us find our forever mate in our first relationship. So it is with animals. Some must experience more than one relationship before finding the one that is meant to be their forever home and their forever family. This was the lesson I learned from Fozzy, and he allowed me to suspend my judgment in regard to those who abandon their animals.

With every rescue dogs we place, we know they are going to a situation that is far better than their last. And we are honored to play the role of matchmaker as we assist each dog in finding "the one."

Wendy

Snow white, soft, and sweet. That was Wendy. A nondescript but pretty shepherd of medium build. Silky-coated and sweet-faced with a pink and brown nose. We didn't know much about her. But like many strays we rescue from the shelters, she was afraid and unsure of who to trust. Exactly one hour after her first adoption event, this gentle girl turned Coastal's world upside down.

It was five o'clock in the evening after a particularly long and hectic adoption event. Exhaustion set in. Defenses were down. Wendy's transporter handed her leash to a volunteer at the kennels where we board some of the dogs. And with the slip of a hand, her leash fell to the ground. Wendy was free, and she knew it. And before anyone could react, she bolted, dodging through the hands and legs of volunteers scrambling to reclaim her.

Volunteers sprang to their cars and combed the area. Three hours later, there was no sign of her. We taped flyers to every visible spot in the area. The search for

Wendy continued. I tried tuning into her.

"Wendy. Please. Stop running."

No response.

"We need to find you. At least don't hide."

No response.

"Please don't be afraid. We're only trying to help you. We'll never let harm come to you."

No response.

Since I couldn't reach her, I sent out daily prayers. On Sunday, we printed and placed more flyers throughout the area. Since she wore a pronged collar and was dragging a leash behind her, we feared she'd get hung up on something and be trapped and defenseless. And we worried about her health. Dogs never come out of high-kill shelters in the best of shape. If we didn't find her, would she face dehydration or starvation? It was imperative we find her.

Hourly updates were posted on our website. And Coastal's community of volunteers brainstormed alternatives through a barrage of emails, coordinating with Animal Control to ensure they turned her back to us if they found her. The response to our flyers was amazing. We had numerous calls into our main line, alerting us to "Wendy sightings."

Sunday night, she was spotted in Elfin Forest, a remote area with dense brush and steep hiking trails several miles from our kennels. Volunteers flocked to the area, searching into the late hours of the night.

On Monday, she was spotted in San Marcos, closer to our kennels but miles away from her Sunday night location. New worries popped up. Aside from lack of food or water or the danger of hanging herself with her leash, how would her body hold up to the mileage she was racking up each day? Was she in danger of being hit by a car?

Tuesday morning, she stopped near a small child. He petted her but didn't grab the leash. She was still free and wandering. We got report after report just blocks from one another. But we were always several steps behind her.

We worked on new strategies. What tactics did Animal Control use to catch dogs? What kind of food should we lure her with? Could we borrow some humane traps from Animal Control? Was her original name something other than Wendy? If so, would she respond to that? Was there another dog at Coastal that she was connected to? One that might give her peace of mind? One that might signal we were here to help?

Wednesday. Two more sightings. Again in San Marcos. New volunteers rushed to the site, hopeful of luring her with food and looked until eleven o'clock that night. Without success. It was like a riveting movie. Those who couldn't join the search stayed glued to their computers for the latest news. Others manned our phone lines and kept volunteers out in the field abreast of new sightings, and we all kept our fingers crossed that we'd find her soon.

Thursday. She was sighted again two times that morning and again at eight o'clock that night. Five volunteers sent responses through email that they were on it. One had been looking since the previous afternoon. Again they continued until late into the night. Again without success.

Friday. Mid-morning. Another sighting in San Marcos, just blocks from where she'd been seen the night before. An hour later, the announcement came back.

We had found Wendy!

The story turned out to be "stranger than fiction." A passerby who had spotted her saw Coastal volunteers putting up flyers. He approached and said he'd seen Wendy resting on a house porch nearby and led them to her. But she took off—and led us around for thirty minutes.

During that time, there were more sightings, and a young man who lived in the area helped our volunteers for a while until they finally lost her again. The young man had to leave the chase, but one of the volunteers handed him a business card, asking him to call if he saw Wendy again.

The man returned to his house a few blocks away. He walked into his bedroom and was shocked to find Wendy taking a nap on his bed! She had entered his house through an open garage door. He closed the door quickly and called us, using the number on our business card. Coastal got to his house swiftly, coaxed Wendy into a crate, and showered her with attention. Then whisked her to the vet for a checkup.

What are the odds that Wendy would enter into the exact house of the same man who had just helped us? It was a stroke of luck that rewarded the tireless efforts of volunteers and the community of San Marcos—a testimony to the hard work of many people.

We celebrated Wendy's safety en masse. Hitting the "Reply to All" key and emailing back and forth furiously.

One volunteer emailed, "Perhaps this young guy would like to adopt Wendy? Fate has intervened. The Gods have spoken. Perhaps he should listen."

Another wrote, "This is a truly touching of story of the kindness of human hearts. So many strangers generously gave their time to help us. Not something you see every day."

And yet another, "Yeah!!!!!! Mega howls for those that helped Wendy!!!!! It was hard to think about what she was going through. I'm so relieved she's safely back with us."

And our fearless leader, Tess, wrote, "That's the latest, guys! And an enormous Aaaaawwwwwhhhhhhoooo to everyone that answered the call for Wendy. People were up late last night talking to our volunteers and trying to track her down. And Wendy is one lucky dog to have all of you behind her!!!!! Coastal Rescue Encinitas always *rocks* the dog world!!!!! Way to go! And yes, I *am* doing the doggie dance!"

The vet examined Wendy and found that her paw pads were worn but not badly. She was given an anti-inflammatory to reduce swelling and pain from a week's worth of running. Surprisingly, she was not as dehydrated as we thought. Nonetheless, we put her on fluids to help her bounce back quicker.

Later that day, volunteers retrieved her from the vet, gave her a bath, and delivered her to a safe, comfortable foster home so she could rest and recuperate in a quiet and peaceful environment.

That night, her new foster dad sent us an email.

"I want everyone to know we have a very tired girl tonight who is resting peacefully and safely here. It would be upsetting to try and contemplate what the days and nights, since last Saturday, must have been like for her. So instead, let's try and focus on a bright new light shining on her life. Thank you all for your support and help in finding her. The two women in San Marcos that spotted her last night in their neighborhood have been called and thanked. They were elated to hear the news! As was the man in San Marcos who found Wendy in his bedroom and alerted one of our volunteers. A truly remarkable set of events that all led up to her being found! I hope you all sleep a little better tonight. I know I will."

Wendy continues to live with her foster dad, Larry. In a twist of fate almost as strange as Wendy's story, Larry had been contacted by a woman who'd seen another stray, a fluffy shepherd mix that appeared in her neighborhood from time to time. The day Wendy came to live with Larry, the stray dog appeared again, Larry was called to the scene, and he successfully captured that dog. Now Wendy and her foster brother, Teddy, a big grey and black woolly mammoth of a guy, live in harmony in their foster home while they search for a home where they can be together forever.

Wendy's story touched me not only because her rescue culminated in a happy ending, but because it illustrates the power of teamwork and community, humbly coalescing to achieve a noble goal through responsibility, diligence, and devotion to a common cause. When we work together, there is little that can't be accomplished.

Sedona

Mother Theresa once said, "A joyful heart is the inevitable result of a heart burning with love." She must have had Sedona in mind. Like so many of our dogs, Sedona was a stray, so we didn't have much background on her. But we quickly learned that Sedona was one of the sweetest dogs we'd ever met. An angel with a heart of gold.

Her time on the streets had left her thin and frail. And along with her heart of gold, Sedona also had a heart condition called pulmonic stenosis, a situation caused when the pulmonary valve is deformed at birth and then fuses shut.

Sendona's heart pumped twice as hard to push blood through the narrow, stiff little valve. As a result, the right side of her heart was thickened from overwork, causing a disturbance in the rhythm of the heart's filling and pumping. Left untreated, it would lead to weakness, lethargy, fainting, and ultimately her death.

And because her heart had been working overtime to pump blood throughout her four years of life, she tired easily. Even eating seemed as if it required too much energy.

We consulted a cardiologist. He recommended a fairly simple surgical procedure called balloon valvuloplasty, a process in which a special balloon is inserted into the pulmonic valve and then inflated, breaking down the obstruction. The procedure would greatly improve her quality of life. And her heart would function normally.

All in all, the cardiologist's diagnosis was promising—and he felt that despite her condition, she was a strong dog. All signs pointed to a positive recovery. And soon after surgery, Sedona could shed her frail and tired shell, gain weight, and develop much-needed muscle strength.

But cardiologists don't come cheap, and the estimate for the procedure and after care totaled $4,000. We need to raise funds fast. No small feat, especially considering the economy. But without this procedure, Sedona would die. This special girl had been fighting hard to live this long, and we couldn't bear to see her lose the battle now.

We appealed to friends, family, and supporters to make tax-deductible donations, large or small. We posted a plea on our website. And we prayed that collectively we could make a difference in her life.

Our prayers were answered, our dreams for Sedona manifested, and her surgery became a reality. And it went off flawlessly. So flawlessly, she was released the following day.

Her post-surgery transformation was like putting a brand new battery in the Energizer Bunny and then trying to restrain it with a rubber band.

Sedona was bursting with life, desperate to use her newly found zeal immediately. Now she had the strength to play with her four-legged siblings. Now she could jump for joy, scale fences, and clear obstacles. Now she could run like a Ferrari with a newly filled tank of gas.

But recovery came first. And Sedona was restrained for two weeks while she healed from surgery. And while Sedona had the patience of Job, the compassion of Mother Theresa, and a heart of gold, she wasn't above playing the guilt card during her two-week recovery. She had the "I'd rather be out there playing with them than in here resting" face down to a T. But orders are orders, and we'd come too far to break the rules now.

The two weeks dragged slowly for Sedona and for her fosters, Sharon and Mike. But finally her post-surgery checkup was scheduled, and she passed with flying colors and wowed the cardiologist and his staff with her newfound vigor and beauty. Although the beauty had always been apparent.

Finally, Sedona received the green light to run and play and frolic. Her only physical limitations would be those she placed on herself. In her doctor's words, "Let Sedona do what Sedona wants to do." Sedona was rarely at an adoption event, since Sharon didn't want to expose her to the stress. So I had to tune into her from afar.

"Sedona. What does it feel like now that your heart is healed?"

Free. Free as a bird. Like I could soar.

"What did it feel like before the surgery? When you tried to run or play?"

Gripping. Like something squeezing my heart.

"What was your last family like?"

Ignorant.

"You mean they didn't know about your condition."

Oh, they knew. Why do you think they abandoned me?

"That happens to a lot of Coastal's dogs. We spend thousands on surgeries that owners can't or don't want to fund. Usually it's hip surgery. You were unique."

Oh.

"What's your favorite thing to do now?"

Play. I'm a clown at heart.

I laughed. "Cute."

And butterflies. I especially like the yellow ones.

Then she drifted out.

Now Sedona lives the normal life of a normal dog. Trips to the dog park. Hours of chasing balls. Days filled with playtime and romps in the yard, where she runs free and strong with other dogs.

Sedona found her forever home in the fall of 2009. She was adopted by Sharon's family, making Sharon a member of what we fondly refer to as the "Failed Foster Club." Sedona now has a family that allows her to be herself and does treat her as an invalid. A home with other dogs who play games with her. A home filled with love, joy, and tranquil moments where she is an integral part of the family routine.

We are incredibly grateful to those who helped give Sedona a second chance at life. Without the commitment of our volunteers, sponsors, benefactors, and steadfast supporters, none of what we do in the rescue work would be possible. Thank you for helping us to give the gift of a new heart and a new life.

Kieffer

I never talked to Kieffer, but from the moment I saw his picture on our website, peeking shyly from behind a yellow daisy bush, mouth open in a happy smile, he stole my heart. What I didn't know was that behind his beautiful smile was a boatload of pain.

According to his foster mom, Kieffer followed her around like a child, looking for approval, eyes begging for a soft and gentle touch. In her words, "All he wants is to be loved." He ran and played with the energy of a typical six-month-old puppy. The only sign that anything was wrong was the leg he dragged behind. But he didn't let that bother him—he loved life too much to let pain stop him.

Kieffer's history would show a different picture. How this beautiful black and tan boy ever ended up on the streets as a stray no one will ever know. Then, upon entering the shelter hungry and disoriented, he was given a bowl of food and promptly sentenced to death for gulping it too quickly.

When Coastal intervened, we knew we were saving a special boy, but we didn't know how special until we discovered his history. We noticed his pronounced limp immediately and the way his right hind leg dragged behind him like dead weight. And we rushed him to the vet. The diagnosis: severe hip luxation.

Not a result of an ailment common to aging shepherds but due to an old pelvic fracture that was ignored by his former owners. But there was far more tragic news. Kieffer also had an injury in his other leg, undoubtedly caused by physical abuse. While he was only a baby, Kieffer had endured more pain and horror than most dogs ever know.

We promised Kieffer a life free of abuse and pain. A life filled with love and joy. He went to one of our loving fosterers and was immediately given medication to numb his pain until we could schedule desperately needed but complicated surgery. Unfortunately for Coastal, Kieffer's plight coincided with Sedona's. Their surgery estimates combined with a few additional procedures totaled $12,000. And it was $12,000 we didn't have. We redoubled our fundraising efforts, posting a plea for donations on our website and exhausting our personal networks to raise the funds.

Kieffer needed a triple pelvic osteotomy (TPO), a complicated procedure used to prevent the severe arthritis of the hips caused by hip dysplasia. The process involved making separate surgical incisions to cut the pelvis in three places: the groin, the rump, and over the side of the hip region. The pelvis would then be rotated the desired amount. Finally, a plate and screws would secure the pelvis in the rotated position, capturing the head of the femur and preventing the joint from popping in and out.

Day by day, dollar by dollar, the donations rolled in. But due to a struggling economy, we were only able to raise one-third of the funds Kieffer needed. The vet who we generally work with was willing to take payments, but unfortunately, he didn't have the necessary background to perform the TPO. Instead, an alternative surgery was considered, and while it would be successful, it would mean that Kieffer would never recover the full range of motion for one leg. Instead, Kieffer's fosters contributed the remaining funds, donating thousands of dollars so Kieffer could have the TPO. It was an unprecedented act of generosity.

Kieffer's surgery was scheduled and performed with precision, and he was able to come home the next day. He lost weight at first. Antibiotics and pain medication made him nauseated, unable to stomach anything other than chicken. But he handled it like a champ. Each day, his appetite increased and his strength surged back.

Although Kieffer was feeling better, he was ordered to be on strict bed rest for the next month and restricted activity for another month. It would be difficult for a spirited puppy, but Kieffer was a remarkably cooperative patient, sporting a stylish plastic cone to prevent him from removing the numerous staples prematurely. One week down, seven more to go.

Kieffer continued to mend in the care of his foster home and was adopted by his fosters in April of 2009, the same family who adopted Maggie. His new family is kind and loving and playful. Just like him. According to his family, Kieffer now runs like a cheetah and leaps like a gazelle.

Kieffer's story remains a testament to the commitment Coastal and its volunteers has to its dogs. Once a dog is in Coastal's care, no expense is spared. No case is too extreme. They simply don't say no. Nor do they give up. Ever. They are quite simply the guardian angels of the dog world.

Pratt

His ears jutted out flat on either side of his head. In fact, you could practically land a plane on the flat runway of his ears. And his bio on Coastal's website made references to flying and his ability to be the perfect copilot to navigate life's experiences. He was uncharacteristically mellow, especially for a two-year-old. But underneath that classic black-and-tan exterior beat the heart of a goofball.

Pratt had been with us for months, an unusually long time for one of our dogs. Generally, unless a dog has issues, they're adopted within a few weeks. Pratt's only flaw was that he didn't get along with other dogs.

At an event in late February, I noticed Pratt had been in a crate for a while. I opened the door, and he was eager to come out. We walked and walked for almost ninety minutes. I kept reminding him that his day would come. That he'd find the perfect family. Every dog in Coastal's care did in time. Each time we'd stop for a break, I'd bend down and put my arm around his shoulders and hug him, pouring love into him. He'd lick my face in response, slow and deliberate.

"I can't believe you're still with us. You're a special puppy. We're going to find you a good home."

I like you. I've never met anyone who could talk.

"Everyone can. They just don't know it."

You're different. I can feel you. I can't feel everyone.

"It's only because I'm open. You can feel my heart."

After a while, we claimed a quiet corner of Coastal's event and sat on the cool tile floor. I slung my arm casually over his shoulders, and we chilled. It's probably my favorite part of handling these dogs. The quiet moments spent relaxing with them. It's when you get to see them. As a handler, you mostly see the top of their backs and the back of their heads and make an impersonal connection at best. It's only when you stop and bend down to hug them or sit and rest with them that you get to see their face, look into their eyes, and interact.

My mind wandered, and I stroked his chest absentmindedly. Mental exhaustion was setting in. And I was beginning to drift into a zone. Pratt took my arm in his teeth, mouthing me gently. I ignored it at first. He was either playing or showing affection. His chewing got harder. I looked at him. Confused. He gnawed in earnest. Like he was teething, and I was a rawhide chew toy.

"Pratt. No." I removed my arm. He went after me again. I put my hands gently around his snout to restrain him.

"Pratt. No." He did it again.

"No," I repeated. As soon as my hands left his nose, he went after my arm again. I stood and avoided his mouth. I knew he wasn't being aggressive. My sense was that he'd just never had anyone talk to him. He'd never felt this connection. Or this energy. Was he so enamored he wanted to consume me? To ingest my energy so he could feel it from the inside out, rather than the outside in? Or was he just being playful? I learned later this was simply one of his quirks. He just liked to chew things—arms, shoes, bedding. He never bit down hard; he just gnawed. And he was notorious for shredding leashes with a single bite.

I walked him outside where the mob of shoppers and foot traffic could divert his attention from my flesh. We sat in the shade, on the cool concrete sidewalk and watched passersby. I positioned myself on a ledge above him. Out of reach from his mouth. A couple approached me. Happy, kind, and probably in their seventies.

"Who's this?" the woman asked.

"Pratt." I responded. "He's two. Sweet boy. Pretty well-mannered."

"Oh, we were looking for an older dog."

"Take him for a walk," I offered. "He's pretty mellow for two."

"We've just started looking," the woman said. "We lost our German shepherd in December."

"I'm sorry. I know what that feels like…. You could still take him for a walk."

The man took the leash, and I walked beside them, threading our way through parked cars and people. Pratt walked calmly at the man's heel. Never once jumping up or pulling on the leash. And they were duly impressed. I could tell Pratt liked the man right away. He leaned into him and licked his hand each time we stopped to chat about his attributes. They were starting to consider him. I walked them back into PetSmart so they could talk to one of our head volunteers about adopting.

I stayed with Pratt and watched their conversation from a distance. I so hoped this might be Pratt's day. But they started looking at other dogs. Then they left. Maybe they would come back next week. Maybe it was too soon for them to commit. I knew they liked Pratt. Maybe they just needed to sleep on it. But they didn't come back.

Like most dogs who come into Coastal's care, Pratt yearns for love and a true connection. He yearns to find a home where his people are devoted to him. And he deserved that. As the weeks passed, I observed Pratt. Up close and from afar.

What I sensed about Pratt is that he had a block. Some sort of mental conditioning from his past that made him put up boundaries or shrouded his imagination. Words like "can't" and "but" corralled his dreams into tight compartments. He could neither see nor visualize his perfect future. And he had no idea he was sabotaging his search. No wonder he'd been with us far longer than most of our dogs. Once I realized this, I asked him why he thought he didn't have a home yet.

I don't know.

"I think it's because you don't know what you want. You need to get clear. If you aren't clear, you can't manifest what you want."

How do I do that?

"Visualize what you want. What kind of family. Older? Younger? Playful? Active? Not so active? Kids? Travelers? Be specific. You can make this happen."

Over the next few days, I'd find time to focus on him and "check in" with him.

"There's an adoption event in two days. Are you visualizing your perfect family?"

I'm making progress.

"Tell me?"

Someone nice. I want them to be kind.

"That's a start."

He was the first dog out of the transport on Saturday. And I was there to greet him. I took his leash and walked him around the back of PetSmart, where we let all the dogs relieve themselves and burn off steam before the event.

Three families had come. Specifically to see him. That was a first. He turned on the charm, sitting on cue, offering a polite paw, and licking hands and chin when they were offered. But they all moved on to look at other dogs. Pratt sank dejectedly by my feet and lay completely flat. I'd never seen him do this, and I could tell he was depressed. He'd given his all to make a good impression on each family. And they'd turned their backs.

"Don't give up. It's early in the event. No one is making any decisions yet."

I'm exhausted. Completely exhausted.

"I understand. But don't give up."

Can you put me in a crate? I need to escape.

I found a crate, plastic with solid sides so he could hide out for a while. Shortly after, I was surprised to see another volunteer walking him. Showing him a second time to one of the families who had come to see him. At the end of the day, I passed by and noticed they were holding Pratt's leash. I asked the woman if they were adopting him. She answered "yes" and beamed from ear to ear.

"He's special," I said. "You're lucky."

"I know. We just adore him."

"Can I say goodbye?" I asked and knelt before him.

"You did it," I said. "You manifested a home."

I did. I had no idea this could be done.

"I heard they have two other dogs. Try to get along. Don't be a pushover. But don't go out of your way to cause problems."

Okay.

Then he walked away with his new family. I hoped it would work, and I wondered if he would in fact mesh with the other dogs. He didn't. By day two, he'd attacked both other dogs in the home and was returned. For everyone's safety.

I walked him at the next event and talked to him.

"I am sorry, puppy. But I told you that you had to get along with the other dogs."

You told me not to be a pushover. Those dogs were idiots. They deserved to be attacked.

"Really? And that was your call?"

They were stinky.

"Praaatt," I admonished. "You gotta be able to go with the flow."

I thought I did.

"Go with the flow means try to get along. Not go with the flow of doing whatever you want."

Oh, right. I get it.

"So we need to find you a home with no dogs."

Not necessarily. They just need to not be idiots.

"I think you've made your point."

Duly noted.

"Don't give up. Keep visualizing what you want. Sometimes it takes time to manifest your dreams. Trust that it will all unfold exactly as it is meant to at exactly the appropriate moment. Timing is everything."

Pratt was with us for two more months. Sometimes he lost hope. Sometimes he'd forget to trust the process. Sometimes I did too. Then I'd remind him again. To continue to visualize. To continue to have hope even though it seemed that we might never find his perfect match. I'd remind him that sometimes the universe's timing isn't in synch with what our ego wants. I'd tell him to continue to hope and to trust the process. I'd remind him that timing is everything.

It was at a mini event, our shorter two-hour events that we hold at our kennels. Sharon poked her head through the kennel door.

"Do you want anyone in particular?" she asked.

"No," I said. My thoughts were elsewhere. Then I paused. "Oh. Wait a minute.

Can you give me Pratt?"

We grinned.

She returned moments later and handed Pratt's leash to me. We walked down the dirt path by the side of the road. He sniffed dead leaves, tracing a trail I couldn't see or smell. We came to a park bench where we sat, free from the chaos of the event. I hugged him, and he leaned into me. I reminded him that today could be the day, and even if it wasn't, we would find his perfect home eventually.

We wandered back to the event and stood on the periphery, elevated a little on top of a small dirt bank. Bushes bursting with yellow flowers bloomed behind us, and I plucked one and threaded it through his collar.

"You need a boutonniere," I teased.

Casey, one of Coastal's leaders, approached us and bent to tousle Pratt's head. Yellow petals scattered on his neck.

"Someone's coming to see you today," he crooned in a thick Australian accent.

"Really? To see Pratt!"

"Yeah. Poor guy lost his dog to cancer a couple of months ago. He's coming to see Pratt and Matrix."

"So he's looking for a challenge then," I said. Casey and I smiled, and he walked away.

A few moments later, I saw Casey point us out, and a portly gentleman, reminiscent of Santa Claus, walked toward us. He had a kind face and a happy smile. But there was pain behind his eyes.

"Is this Pratt?" he asked.

"Yes. I understand you've come to meet him and Matrix."

"I have. Can you tell me about him?"

"Sure. I handle him a lot. He's between two and a half and three years old. Great temperament. Easy-going. Mellow. Great on a leash. Loves people. He just doesn't get along with other dogs. He's not aggressive on-leash. Just off-leash. Oh…and he chews things. Never hard… but you need to watch him. Want to take him for a walk?"

"Sure."

We threaded our way through the jumble of dogs and handlers, cars, and would-be clients, and I handed him the leash. I gave him a few pointers and continued to talk up Pratt's good qualities. We sat on a park bench. Where I'd given Pratt the pep talk earlier. He patted Pratt and ran his hand over his coat, speaking softly to him. Pratt leaned into him and licked his chin. The man's eyes welled with tears. Then he uttered the words that Pratt and I and at least a dozen Coastal volunteers had yearned to hear for months.

"Well, pal, I think you may be the one."

Pratt got adopted that day. To a perfect home where he is the only perfect dog. Timing *is* everything.

It occurred to me that Pratt was perhaps the poster child for *The Secret*—the powerful bestselling book offering advice about visualizing and creating the life of your dreams. Pratt is a reminder that each of us has the power to make our hopes and dreams a reality. We just need to put it out there and trust the process and the universe's timing with deep faith.

Pratt embodies the symbolic power of perseverance. Even though he wanted to give up, week after week, he continued to give his dream one more shot. He is manifestation and trust at its finest.

Ollie

Ignorance. It's all around us. In the humans who abuse or neglect an animal. In the parents who let their children run rampant at our rescue events, charging headlong into our dogs and sticking fingers into crates. In the clueless owners who bring their tiny toy dogs into PetSmart and let them wander aimlessly on a thirty-foot leash while we attempt to restrain a hundred-pound shepherd from helping itself to a snack. In the would-be adopters who attempt to "train" one of our dogs to sit or lie down without knowing their background. In the humans who feed too much, or too little, or confine their canine family member solely in a backyard. And it's in the well-intentioned advice of those who truly haven't all the facts. I should know. I've made plenty of mistakes myself, all out of ignorance.

I could retire tomorrow, a wealthy woman, if I had a dime for every time I said, "Sir, please don't push his haunches like that. You're not alpha in his mind yet. He's not going to sit for you just yet." Or "Miss, please don't let your child put his fingers through the crate.

Our dog might think it's food." Or "Offer him the back of your hand first. Don't reach over his head. *Please*! I said *don't* reach over his head. Pat his shoulder. That's better." Most people are well-intentioned. They don't intend to be ignorant. But they are.

Ignorance was especially apparent the day I walked Ollie. Randy, a fellow volunteer, had yelled to me across the parking lot, asking if I'd met Ollie. He knew my weakness for big, classic, black-and-tan alpha males.

I'd not even heard of Ollie, so I entered our adoption area and peered into several crates, looking at the names stenciled on bandanas that our dogs wear around their necks. Then I found him and opened his crate. He rose slowly, uncoiling the full extent of his immense build. My eyes widened, and I caught my breath. I hoped he'd be easy to handle. I grabbed his leash, took him out of his crate, and sized him up. He was a dramatic, dark black-and-tan. Bold, regal, and cool. His stature was almost godlike.

"Ohhhh, you are my type," I said. "You are magnificent."

I took him outside for a spin. When we rounded the corner to the back of the store, I knelt and hugged him. A voice in the back of my head whispered, you don't know him, it might not be a good idea to be down on his level. I ignored it. To my surprise, he licked my chin and then dropped and rolled to his back, inviting a tummy rub.

"What a shweetie bug you are," I said, giving his belly a vigorous scratch.

And he *was* a love. Sweet, eager to please, and kind.

Since he was new, he needed a photo for our website. He and I posed dutifully while another volunteer snapped photo after photo. Ollie played to the camera, licking my face, leaning into me, and rolling on his back again as if to say that despite his beefcake good looks, and commanding size, he had a goofy, submissive side as well.

Once he was captured for posterity, we resumed our walk, strolling casually along the rough-hewn block wall that was partially hidden by climbing vines. We sauntered through flower beds carpeted with thick green ground cover and low-growing yellow daisies. Then we wandered slowly back to the wide sidewalk in front the store.

One of our volunteers passed by with another dog. Ollie went off, barking voraciously. I looked at him in confusion. Was the volunteer fostering him? Was he trying to get her attention? Or was it the other dog he wanted?

"It's okay. Don't worry."

No answer.

"Tell me what's wrong."

No answer.

I gave up trying to connect and turned my focus on what to do next. Should I follow the volunteer who'd set him off or turn around and attempt to divert his attention? Whatever I did, I needed to be careful. I'd only handled Ollie for about ten minutes. Not enough time to establish alpha or authority with this boy. And he was distraught. If I corrected him too heavily, he could turn his aggression on me.

Instinct kicked in. Handle him delicately. I pulled gingerly on the leash, cueing him to change direction. He followed me but craned his neck, continuing to bark at the female volunteer and her dog as they disappeared around the corner of the building. I changed tactics, and decided to try a series of subtle zigzag direction changes to get his mind refocused him on me. Two steps to the right, three to the left, back and forth. It wasn't working. I turned full circle and headed toward PetSmart's front doors. Ollie barked furiously at everything and everyone.

An employee from some beauty store I can't remember the name of watched us as she lounged on a bench, taking a break. A cigarette dangled from her fingers. She wore a burgundy polo shirt and jeans, and her hair was swept up in an unkempt ponytail.

"Ma'am!" she yelled. "You need to have a firmer hand with him. Yank on his leash. Get him to stop barking."

Ignorance at its finest.

Nine months of averting dog fights, nine months of keeping whatever dog I was handling from snatching up a poodle in its jaws while its owner obliviously scanned the shelves for today's sale item, nine months of patient admonishments to ignorant lookey-loos all culminated in one perfect road-rage moment, and I snapped.

"Using a heavy hand is *not* my style. And even if it *was*, this dog is new to us. I am *hardly* an authority figure in his mind. You *clearly* don't have a clue. So back off!"

Blood pounded in my head. Ignorance is *not* bliss.

Then I shot a withering look her way and led Ollie into the store. He continued to bark, even in the store. This dog was not going to settle, and I could not pacify him.

I saw an open crate in our adoption space and surrendered him to its safety. Instantly, he quieted. And I sought one of our adoption counselors, to share the story and ask advice.

"Should I have done something differently?" I asked.

"Dobie," she admonished, "always trust your instincts. Ollie's only been back with us for three days. We know *nothing* about what happened while he was gone. You did the right thing."

"What do you mean back? I thought he was new."

"He was with us awhile back. Owner turn-in. They lost their house, and now the woman has cancer. They were broken-hearted to lose him."

"*I* never saw him. How could I miss a guy like him?"

"He came in and was adopted the same day. I think you were in Lake Tahoe."

"Oh. Right. Why did he come back?"

"I heard he attacked someone."

Always trust your instincts.

Later that day, I found the woman that had originally set Ollie off. "Are you fostering him?" I asked.

"No. I was as surprised as you. I don't know what set him off."

It was a mystery. She wasn't his foster mom. He hadn't been with us long enough to make that kind of connection with any of our other dogs. What had caused his distress?

At the end of the day, I took Ollie out of his crate and walked him outside to a quiet area.

"What happened out there?"

I was mad.

"Why?"

Something was there that I couldn't see. Didn't know.

"What? What was it?"

I don't know. It felt funny.

"Were you scared?"

I was protecting you. That's what shepherds do.

"But from what?"

I told you. Something I couldn't see. I could only feel it. Bad energy.

"Like a ghost?"

Not a ghost. Something different. It didn't feel safe.

"Would it have harmed us?"

Not sure. Wasn't taking chances.

"Thank you."

You're welcome.

And so it is with shepherds. They guard, tend, and guide us. They watch over and protect. They shield us from danger or harm. They are guardian angels for those they love. Sometimes even for those they barely know.

The following Saturday morning, I checked email, wondering who I'd be transporting to the event that day. I smiled. I was transporting Ollie.

I stood outside our kennels in San Marcos with the other volunteers, each of us waiting for the dog we were to transport that day. And while I waited, I learned more about Ollie. He'd been relinquished to us about two months prior. Until then, he'd lived with his human family since he was eight weeks old. Sadly, Ollie's human mom was diagnosed with cancer and then was evicted from her rental home when the landlord stopped paying the mortgage without her knowledge. Since the family he'd lived with for five years was homeless, so was he. She turned to Coastal, hoping that we could take him in and find a suitable home. Ollie was quickly adopted and lived with his new family for about a month.

But he'd rattled his new people when he growled at a big, strange man dressed in black who had approached them during a walk. And they'd turned him back to us, saying he was too aggressive. He wasn't aggressive. He'd only been protecting his people from something he'd thought presented danger. That's what shepherds do. But his new people weren't equipped to handle him, so they returned him. It was for the best.

Moments later, Ollie emerged from the kennels and wagged his tail in recognition. I scooped him up and headed out for a brisk walk so he could burn off some steam and relieve himself before the car ride to PetSmart.

Once we were in the car, he whined nervously during the entire ride. I talked to him in soothing tones trying to settle him. Occasionally he'd lick my face. Once he tried to climb in the front seat.

"No!" I commanded and placed my arm to block him. He complied and settled in the back seat. But he knew the route to PetSmart and rose when we approached the final stoplight before turning into the parking lot. He began whining again.

"Are you excited?"

No answer.

"Nervous?"

No answer.

"Don't worry. We're going to find you the perfect home."

I parked and opened his door, and he leapt out of the car. I grabbed his leash, skirted rows of parked cars, and headed toward the main sidewalk and then around the corner. It was a cool summer morning. Fog was just beginning to burn off, and Ollie had tons of energy. We began to jog. Despite his size, Ollie was surprisingly light on his feet, and I was soon out of breath.

Later, we chilled on the grass in front of the store. A couple approached. She was athletic. Her soft, red hair was cut in a medium-length pageboy, and freckles faintly peppered her cheeks. He was medium build and tanned with close-cropped silver hair and blue eyes.

"Are you with the rescue?" she asked.

"I am." I screened my eyes from the sun with my hand, looked up at her and smiled.

"Who's this?"

"Ollie. He's five. Super boy."

"Ollie! We *came* to see Ollie."

"Awesome," I said, and I stood to shake their hands. Then I gave them the rundown on him.

"Do you have experience with shepherds?" I asked.

"Yes. Our last one, big white guy, just passed away," he said.

"I'm sorry. I know what that feels like."

"Yeah. It's not easy."

"Have you been to our website?"

"Yes. Every day for several weeks," she answered.

"So you know our criteria. Fenced yard. Dog is a part of the family, not banished to the backyard."

"Yes, of course. That's how we raised our shepherd."

We continued to talk. They seemed ideal. She ran with her dog daily. He'd trained dogs in the military. He worked from home. They had a huge fenced yard. They were kind, compassionate people who'd give any dog the love, structure, and leadership that was needed. I handed her Ollie's leash and accompanied them on a walk. Then I introduced them to several other dogs I thought might be a fit. We spent almost an hour together as I gave them the details about our dogs and introduced them to Tess, our leader, for a final screening.

I thought they might adopt that day, but they wanted to think about it, and I agreed. It's not a decision to be made lightly. I gave them my cell phone number so they could bypass Coastal's answering service in case they wanted to call about Ollie or Booker, the other dog they'd been drawn to.

The next day, I had a call. They'd chosen Ollie. They'd chosen well.

My time with Ollie was brief, but it was also profound. For me, Ollie was a strong reminder to trust your gut in any situation. He is a strong reminder to pay attention to your surroundings and to stay alert and present and in the moment. He was a strong reminder not to judge people or situations, because you might not know the big picture. He is a reminder not to offer advice unless it is asked for. Most importantly, he is a reminder not to tell others what to do especially if you don't have all the facts because to do so is to come from a place of ignorance. And ignorance is not bliss.

Murphy

I never met Murphy. He was before my time at Coastal. But his story is too special not to be shared. He was a gentle dog. Two to three years of age. A motley black and red German shepherd, suffering from scabies — a treatable condition that his people found easier to ignore.

Worse, they confined him to the backyard. Chained to a tree. With just enough food to keep him alive. They ignored his medical needs. They ignored his physical needs. They ignored pretty much everything.

A kind neighbor stepped in and reported Murphy's people. He was immediately impounded and brought to the animal shelter. Unfortunately for him, his time was running out, and he was put on the euthanize list because of his condition. He was on his last twenty-four hours when Coastal got the call. It was then that life began anew for Murphy. When we picked him up, he greeted his rescuers with kisses.

By the time Coastal rescued Murphy, his face and

stomach were bald and exposed and his legs were protected by only sparse tufts of fur. And he was scrawny and malnourished. This was not something that happened overnight. Murphy had suffered for a long time.

Murphy was boarded in Coastal's kennels because of the shortage of foster homes. And on his first day, he received his first bath in what appeared to be a very long time. He loved it. What was left of his matted fur was brushed, and it was absolutely gorgeous.

He savored long walks with caring volunteers. He delighted in carrying toys in his mouth. If none were available, he was only too happy to pick up a stick and carry that. If you sat down, he'd stop and double back, eager to give hugs or lie down in your lap.

Murphy was a simple, gentle dog with simple needs. It didn't seem to bother him that he didn't look like our other dogs. He didn't seem to mind that his beautiful coat was patchy and sparse. Maybe he knew that he was truly beautiful from the inside out.

I think that in coming to Coastal, Murphy knew he had a shot at a new home and a new start. Although I never met Murphy, I sensed that his innocence and imagination carried him on his journey. He embraced his doubts and fears and did not let the past foreshadow his future.

Murphy was adopted long before I joined Coastal and has, from what I hear, since grown into a stunning dog. His outer beauty now mirrors his inner beauty. Gone are the chains, the abuse, and the hunger of his past. He lives with a wonderful man and will never again want for food, or safety, or shelter. His life is filled with simple pleasures, hope, and a true partnership. And most important of all...love.

Murphy's story reminds me of a little film called *Fish*. It documents a day at the famous Pike Place Fish Market in Seattle and one special vendor. What makes this vendor unique is that, like Murphy, the employees begin each day by choosing their attitude. They choose to be upbeat, funny, and joyful. They play with their customers and toss fish around, shouting and yelling and spreading cheer, a mood that they inspire others to adopt. That is Murphy's gift to us. He invites us to choose our attitude, and in doing so, we shape our existence and help others to do the same.

Eddie

Once in a great while, one slips through the cracks and for whatever reason, we can't save them. Their life takes a turn that we don't foresee and therefore can't alter.

Eddie was a lean black and tan male with a narrow snout, soft eyes, and a gentle spirit. Only the dusting of snowy white on his muzzle hinted that he was older. When he came to us, he was shell-shocked. Our first impression was that he was seriously ill. His urine was almost black, and we feared he might be in renal failure. Then we learned the truth.

Eddie had been quarantined in the shelter. Since many of the staff feared German shepherds, he hadn't been walked since he'd arrived. What they didn't know was that Eddie refused to urinate in his enclosure. Instead, he'd held his urine for three days. To add insult to injury, he also had a nasty case of pneumonia.

I read his story in an email from our leader asking for foster homes for several of the week's newly rescued group. And I broke down and cried. I was leaving town for the weekend, but my daughter and I agreed that if Eddie still needed a foster home when I returned, we'd take him and nurse him back to health

Instead, my dear friend Vanessa snatched Eddie up. She lives with two beautiful shepherds and is a Coastal veteran and a skilled caregiver. Eddie was in good hands, and within two weeks, he'd mended physically. But his emotional recovery would take longer, so Vanessa went to work repairing his heart and his soul. It would take weeks for his worried look to yield to happiness. Weeks before he settled into a more comfortable routine. Weeks before he could trust his new environment. But slowly she won him over, and soon he would greet her each morning by bounding into her bed, covering her face with lavish kisses.

When he settled in, he spent his days in the relaxed, amiable companionship of his foster siblings, Sidney and Hannah, and his nights curled up by Vanessa's feet. He had all the comforts any dog could want while he waited to find his forever home.

Eddie was a stately, elegant gentleman. Had he been human, one might have expected to see him lounging in a sumptuous leather chair, adorned in a silk smoking jacket, balancing a snifter of aged cognac in one hand and a premium cigar in the other.

But he had a couple of endearing quirks. He circled obsessively around small objects like coffee tables and footstools. Going round and round as fast as he could.

He'd do the same in confined spaces, a holdover from being confined in a dog run or kennel.

He had a spot at the base of his tail—a special itchy spot that when scratched would trigger both hind legs to pump simultaneously like he was riding a bicycle.

Weeks passed, and no home materialized. Vanessa was seriously considering making her home a permanent stop for this special boy.

On July 3, she came home from an evening out with a friend and opened her patio door to call the dogs. Two came running. Where was the third? She kept counting heads over and over in disbelief. One. Two. Sidney. Hannah. Where was Eddie?

Was he sick? She grabbed a flashlight and patrolled her backyard, lifting limbs and peering under bushes. No sign of Eddie. Had someone taken him? But why would someone steal him and not the other dogs?

When she couldn't find him, she feared that pre–Fourth of July fireworks had spooked him and he'd scaled her six-foot fence either to escape or to look for her.

Overwhelmed with fear, she placed frantic calls to everyone who sprang to mind. Then she jumped in her car and took to the streets for hours in hopes of finding him.

At midnight, the call came. Eddie had dashed into the street and been struck by a car. The driver hadn't even stopped.

Instead, a kind woman, a witness to the accident, stopped her car, got out, and held Eddie in her arms, praying for him until the sheriff arrived. Eddie died in her arms.

Caron and I visited Vanessa the next day. We brought cold beer and fat burritos and sat at her kitchen table, talking, crying, and remembering Eddie. I think it was a comfort to us all that he'd not died alone.

When we left, she walked us to the door and said, "I didn't sleep last night, and as I paced the floor, I knew you guys would come." We hugged tearfully and said our goodbyes.

I went to Eddie with Vanessa's permission.

"Are you still here?"

No. I crossed over.

"You're safe then?"

Yes.

"Would you like to tell Vanessa anything?"

I will love her forever.

"I think I know, but tell me why?"

There were so many "firsts" with her. Before her, I never really played. I never understood or felt unconditional love. I was never part of a pack that accepted me.

"That is special."

She made a difference in my life, and I will love her forever.

Sometimes it is the simplest of things that make a world of difference. There's a fable about a little boy who is playing in the sand on a bay where hundreds of starfish are beached and stranded. The boy stoops, painstakingly plucks a starfish from the sand and lovingly places it back in the water. He does this repeatedly while a man watches from a distance. Finally, the man approaches the little boy.

"Son," he asked, "what are you doing?"

"I'm putting them back in the water," the little boy replied.

"But, son, there are hundreds. You can't possibly think that you can make a difference."

The little boy stared directly into the man's eyes, picked up another starfish, and placed it deliberately into the water. He turned back to the man and said, "I bet I made a difference to that one."

Eddie spent only ten weeks with Vanessa, yet she made a profound difference in his life. Through her simple and deliberate acts of kindness, her loving touch, and her willingness to integrate him into family, Eddie healed and came to know great love and great joy. And because of that he will love her forever.

Eddie's search for his forever home ended on July 3, 2009. But he will live forever in Vanessa's heart. Rest in peace, beautiful boy. Know that you are loved and that you are missed.

Matrix

He can clear a six-foot fence in a single leap and escape from a secure crate in a New York minute. This Houdini of the canine world is as complex as they come.

One of our larger alpha males, Matrix makes many of our dogs look anemic in comparison. His deep, square muzzle and steely, penetrating eyes embody an unwavering will that borders on belligerence. He dares you to be his equal. Carved, muscled shoulders and thick haunches hint that Matrix's outer strength matches his inner resolve.

Unlike Eddie, had Matrix been human he would have been a cross between Clint Eastwood and Marlon Brando. He'd be decked out in black leather and inked with ornate tattoos. A rifle would hang casually over one shoulder, and he'd ride in on a Harley taunting, "Go ahead. Make…my…day."

Quite simply, Matrix is a rebel. For that reason, he was with us for more than a year while we tried to find the perfect home for him.

Three things soften Matrix's bold persona: one ear that is endearingly tipped, a beautiful black and tan coat that is rich and soft and luxuriantly glossy, and the special place he has in his heart for one special volunteer— Jess.

The day Caron asked me to get a read on Klaus, she asked me to do the same with Matrix.

"What happened to you?" I asked Matrix.

My people left me.

"Do you miss them?"

I did. I am happy now because I have hope, but I was broken-hearted about being abandoned.

"What kind of family do you want now?"

A large house and a yard with lots of room. I need a tall fence, or I'll get in trouble. I want a smart person.... I am smart, and my people should be too or I will be bored with them.

"Anything else?"

Tender loving care. And lots of balls...even big ones.

Suddenly, I saw a vision of him sort of playing volleyball or tetherball, chasing a big ball and bouncing it off his nose.

I'd like to be with a man and do manly things, like hiking and be outdoors and even camp with my "person." I could be good with a woman too, but she has to be smart and strong and like the outdoors...and not be afraid to get dirty. And she would have to know how to be an authority figure. I'll be good with someone I respect, but I have high standards for humans because of what I have been through. My respect will not be won overnight.

Are you good with other dogs?

Not really.

"Cats?"

Definitely not.

"Kids?"

Not little ones.

"So an adult-only home then."

Older kids could visit.

I reported back to Caron.

"Well, that fits," she said. "In his bio, we put down that he's large and thinks he's in charge."

"That's why he needs a smart person. One who can provide leadership but with compassion not force."

But Matrix is too intimidating for most. I didn't handle him much at our events because beyond our initial conversation, I don't feel that I can reach him. There are only about two people in our rescue besides Jess who he is connected to.

Jess is numero uno for Matrix. She rescued Matrix from the shelter, and he adores her. In fact, the only time I really see him light up is when Jess is within his view. Then he comes to life with the joy of a young pup. The second is Rob, a tall, sinewy figure of a man who walks Matrix religiously several times a week. Rob loves Matrix but is quick to tell you he is chopped liver in Jess's presence. The third is Bart, who has a way with the difficult dogs and devotes time each week to take kenneled dogs on special field trips where they hike, run on the beach, share time in a therapy pool, or simply explore.

At a mini-event, the short, two-hour events we host at our kennels, Rob was handling Matrix. It was a warm autumn morning, and I wandered through people and dogs. Matrix was fixated on Jess, who was talking to some prospects across the dirt parking lot. He wanted Jess's attention, so he barked incessantly. Rob tried to shush him, but Matrix ignored his cues. I thought that since I'd connected with Matrix, perhaps I could help calm him. I walked up behind Rob and put my hand on Matrix's side, hoping my touch would soothe him. Matrix whipped his head around; his mouth was open, and his eyes fixed on my hand. I froze. Then he looked up at me.

Oh. It's you. I'm busy. His tone was flat and bordering on annoyed. I had been dismissed.

I removed my hand.

I have handled Matrix a couple of times since. He's not aggressive with humans, but he can be with other dogs. For that reason, he wears a red "danger" scarf at our events. The day I did handle him, we didn't connect. He was quietly but diligently focused on other dogs being walked. Watching them with hawk-like eyes, tracking their every move. We try to divert him when he does this so he doesn't get fixated on other dogs, because that's when problems can arise. But even after an hour, talking to him, soothing him, petting him, I doubt he knew there was a human at the end of his leash. He had no interest in connecting with me. I was simply a means to an end.

At another event, I removed him from his crate to tie his bandanna around his neck. Once out of his crate, he fixated on something with a cool, calculated stare. I didn't know what he was looking at and motioned him back into his crate. He stood his ground and didn't move.

"Matrix," I said, pulling his leash to lead him back into the crate, "you need to get back in."

No response. He stood frozen, staring down the aisle.

I tried again, this time pulling gently on the leash and pushing his haunches with my other hand. Again, without success. If he is *this* fixated, I thought, and I try to break his concentration, he might turn on me. I could feel fear, fingering its way into my gut, then the realization that he would sense it and use it to his advantage.

"Vanessa," I yelled out over the din of the event, "can you come help me get Matrix in his crate?" Vanessa walked over and took the leash from me. She tried to maneuver his shoulders. I leaned into his haunches and pushed gently to get him unhinged and moving. He didn't budge. We tried again. He stood his ground. We tried again. Nothing happened.

"Where's Rob or Jess when we need them?" Vanessa muttered under her breath. "Matrix, IN. NOW." She raised her voice. No response. We tried again. Nothing. "What about a treat?" I asked.

"Good idea," she said and pulled a treat out of her fanny pack, handing it to me. I held it in front of his nose so he could get the scent and then walked to the back of the crate and poked it though the bars to entice him to enter. He turned and looked at me but made no indication that he would enter the crate. Vanessa shoved him from behind. He stood frozen. She and I stared at one another, shaking out heads. Suddenly, he walked into the crate but ignored the treat. We rolled our eyes and moved on to attend to other tasks.

I asked her later if she was scared too. She shot me a sidelong glance and looked away. "Yes," she replied, "but I wasn't going to admit it." I nodded and smiled.

One morning, I started up my computer and opened my email. There was a message from our leader, Tess, and the subject line was "Matrix." He was going into a foster-to-adopt home. His new people knew all his issues, but they were willing to work with him. Tess's email continued:

This is the perfect home for our boy. The dad goes to work early, and the mom takes Matrix for a run before she leaves for work mid-morning. Dad comes home at noon, has lunch with Matrix and takes him out for a walk and goes back to work. Then dad comes home around 3:00 to 4:00 p.m. So Matrix is rarely alone. They'll keep him crated while they are gone so he doesn't get into mischief. Keep your paws crossed that this all goes well. They are willing to take one day at a time and take things slowly with our special guy.

I pushed my chair away from the computer and found my daughter. "Matrix went to a foster-to-adopt!"

"No way!"

"Yes. I just got an email from Tess."

"That's amazing, Mom. So cool."

"I know. I'm elated. I didn't think this could ever happen."

A week later, we got another update, via email from Tess. The subject line—"Matrix Update." The email read:

So how's our boy doing, you ask? Here's the rundown on Matrix's first week. Chapter one. First work day. Mom goes out for a light jog and she and Matrix have breakfast together, then she goes to work. Dad comes home for lunch and finds the living room is a mess. Papers are strewn on the floor, file folders are everywhere, envelopes and stamps litter the room. Dad is confused.

Then Matrix comes trotting down the stairs. Dad thinks that Mom is home since the dog is loose, so he calls out to her. No answer, but he hears what sounds like white noise from the TV coming from upstairs, so he and Matrix climb the stairs. No wife. But the water in the tub is running full blast.

Dad's only conclusion is that Matrix had escaped from his crate and played around. Thank goodness the water trap in the tub was open.

Guess Matrix must have thought that he would help his new people by re-organizing their filing system and cleaning the tub. So Dad takes Matrix for a walk, has lunch with him, and puts him back in his crate and goes back to work.

Chapter two. Dad comes home from work at four in the afternoon. Opens door. Matrix is loose again. No damage this time, just a ton of nose prints on the bedroom mirror. Guess our boy discovered that he was one handsome piece of beefcake because he must have spent the afternoon admiring himself in the mirror and singing "I'm too sexy for my fur." The good news is that the whole time Dad is on the phone telling me all this, he is laughing.

His one bad habit from what I hear is counter-surfing. Lots of our dogs do this...they cruise the edge of the kitchen counters to see if they can reach the food. Well, when I say Matrix counter-surfs...I mean on all fours. We all know this guy can jump. According to his people, Matrix jumps up on the counter tops...on all fours!

Tomorrow they are going to try just leaving Matrix uncrated to see how that goes. I've given them pointers about how to make that work. Everyone, keep your paws crossed that Matrix can find his routine with these kind folks.

A week later, we had another email from Tess. Matrix was coming back. He wasn't making progress. He was still counter-surfing. He was destroying their doors with his incessant scratching. But they had done their best and had given Matrix two weeks in their home and a break from his usual routine. And now we knew more about how he'd do in a home environment. So we could equip the next family with more information.

On Saturday, his foster mom brought him back to the kennels during our mini-event. I watched her as she walked him in and then went back to her car to get the paperwork she'd left there. She was visibly distraught. You could see it, even though she wore sunglasses to shield her emotion. It was clear that she'd connected deeply with him and this was not a decision she'd made lightly. I knew her pain. It was what I experienced when I returned Gavin. Matrix seemed fine.

I commented to Vanessa that I was sorry he'd had to come back. He'd been in our kennels so long that I wondered what he thought of that life. Would he have been better off if his position on death row in the shelter hadn't been interrupted?

"You know," Vanessa observed, "I don't think that he thinks the kennels are such a bad deal. He's comfortable. He's got a warm bed and all the food he can eat. He sees Jess and Rob every day. Jess takes naps with him on his dog bed and plays with him all time.

Rob walks him five days a week, and Bart takes him for field trips. Look at his demeanor. He's not sad or lonely. He's loving life."

I thought about what she had said and realized she was right. Matrix is the epitome of emotional and physical health. He is full of life.

It's true that Matrix hasn't been easy to place. Nor is he an easy foster. As he indicated, if he's left alone too long he escapes to look for his people. And Rob believes that he could even clear an eight-foot fence. So he needed a home with a taller-than-average fence, a secure crate, no other dogs, no kids, and definitely no cats. Most people who adopt from us aren't looking for that kind of challenge. So Matrix stayed at our kennels with about twenty or so other dogs.

And even though he and Pratt and Klaus had been with us far longer than any of our other dogs, Pratt had found a home, so why couldn't Matrix? And if Klaus could find a long-term foster and then a home, why not Matrix? It would all happen when the timing was right.

I went to him after he was returned.

"Are you sad it didn't work out?"

It wasn't the right home for me.

"What makes you say that?"

I need a home where they don't care if things are out of place.

"Did you like the people?"

Pretty much.

"The woman seemed pretty connected to you."

She was nice.

"But you don't attach easily, do you?"

I think you know the answer to that.

I retreated from the conversation and pondered what Matrix was here to teach us. What I see in him is that beneath his bad-to-the-bone exterior lies a proud soul. Not the type of pride that is overly done. Nor the kind of pride that interferes with the ability to forgive and accept help or support. But the kind of pride that seems to say, "No matter what has happened in my past, I will not let it crush my spirit nor rob me of my zest for life. I will live with zealous intent. And I will make the most of every moment. No matter what."

Matrix is a rebel. But he is a rebel *with* a cause.

I wondered about Matrix's fascination with his reflection in the mirror. It may have been the first time he had seen himself that clearly. Buddhists believe that one's reflection is a vital part of the soul and that reflective surfaces offer a doorway to the spiritual world, allowing the soul to seek deeper meaning about one's existence. Maybe in that moment of self-admiration, Matrix was coming face to face with his true self for the very first time — and recognizing the potential of the sacred beauty of the soul. More likely, he was simply spending the afternoon *his* way — having fun, walkin' on the wild side, and in the famous words of Will Smith, "gettin' jiggy wit it."

Matrix was adopted several weeks later. This time, it stuck. The mom was an artist and worked from home, so our boy would never have to roam the house looking for his people and deciding to rearrange the filing system instead. Mom also loved hiking and would provide enough activity to keep Matrix off the counter tops. After more than eighteen months of searching, Matrix has found his forever home.

Rohan

"Guess who my new love is," I said to Vanessa.

"Who?" She asked, looking up from the shrimp pizza she was assembling.

"Rohan." I took a sip of wine.

"Of *course* he is." We shared a knowing look and laughed.

"Who's Rohan?" Caron asked. She'd been on hiatus from Coastal for weeks, trying to get her house ready to sell.

"Our new resident alpha male," Vanessa answered. "You know Dobie's type. Black and tan. Alpha male. Stunningly handsome. Classic. *Prey drive*."

"This one would eat my cats for sure. It's like he's *born* to hunt," I said.

Rohan is a beauty. A classic black and tan. Sharp eyes, keen ears, and laser-focused attention. Not a fiber of him was slack or out of place, and his lean, spare frame looked like it was made to run on high-octane fuel.

I was the one of the first at Coastal to meet Rohan when he came to his initial adoption event. Sharon asked me to join her with the dog I was currently walking.

"I want to see how he reacts to other dogs," she explained.

"What's his story?" I asked.

"Owner turn-in. They called us because he bit their teenage son."

"That seems odd. Shepherds don't usually turn on a family member."

"No. They don't. Not if they're socialized properly," she agreed.

"What else do you know?" I asked.

Sharon shared Rohan's story while we walked. The family had wanted an outside guard dog, so Rohan had lived outside, patrolling the perimeter of their fenced land. They did little training with him. And Rohan became aggressive.

It's my pet peeve. No pun intended. These people who get a shepherd because they want an outside guard dog, don't work with them, don't establish boundaries, don't integrate them with the family, and then wonder what went wrong when the dog becomes aggressive. Shepherds bond deeply with their families, and they become overprotective if they're not trained or socialized well. During a rough play session with the teenage son, Rohan had yelped in pain, the boy didn't let go, and Rohan had turned on him out of self-defense.

"How long did they have him?" I asked, dodging several people exiting Albertsons as we walked past.

"Well, he's three. And I think he's been with them for most of his life."

"If Rohan had truly bonded with the family," I said, "I doubt he would have turned on the boy. I played rough with my dog. If his teeth ever grazed me, it was an accident and he would immediately show remorse."

"Exactly. So when I went to see him," she continued, "I met Rohan and the dad at a park. I brought my husband in case Rohan was too much for me to handle.

"And Rohan was good with you?" We stopped, and I leaned down to pet the dog I was handling and offered Rohan the back of my hand. He sniffed it casually and then jerked his head to look at a tiny Chihuahua sporting a tinkling bell on its collar.

"He was great. But, frankly, he came to us just in time. A few more years and it would have been harder to turn him around."

We walked in silence, stopping occasionally to stroke our dogs.

"Since we're stopped, let's let him meet her," she said, cocking her head toward my dog. "I want to see how he does."

I turned my dog's butt to them, the classic dog introduction stance. Sharon gave Rohan some slack on the leash. He lunged at my dog, ramming her butt with his nose. She jumped and spun.

"Looks like he needs to acquire a little more finesse for his meet-and-greets," Sharon said. We grinned.

"She doesn't want you to meet her that way," Sharon said, bending to adjust Rohan's collar. "Let's walk on."

We continued to walk, stopping several more times to let the dogs sniff one another. He made improvements, but he was still a little overzealous. Despite his lack of manners, he was a stunning boy. He had the look of a purebred and appeared to be born to hunt and guard. I knew he would not be adopted quickly. And I knew I would bond with him. But I didn't know if he would bond with me. I do love a challenge, though, so I walked him often at the events I attended.

The first time I walked him by myself, we circled around the entire strip mall. One loop is about half a mile. We clipped along at a brisk pace, but he didn't interact with me. Most dogs will turn from time to time and jump on you or sit and ask for attention. Not Rohan.

Halfway through our second loop, he slowed his pace. I found a grassy, shady spot to sit and pet him. But he wouldn't connect with me. He wouldn't even sit. He paced in circles around me, tracking the movement of cars and people with a piercing focus. Like he was hyper-aware of even the most subtle nuance and shift in his environment. As I watched him, I tried to tune into him.

"Rohan, how are you doing? I mean with all this change and not being with your family?"

No response.

"Are you sad?"

No response.

"Is there anything you want me to know?"

No response.

He continued to pace, then stop and stare, and pace again. Over and over. It was almost like he was a shark and if he stopped moving he'd perish from lack of oxygen. So I stood, and we walked on, making another lap around the mall, more slowly this time. After another thirty minutes, I felt he could use a break, so I gave him some water and put him in a crate with a thick, soft blanket.

At the end of the event, Rohan was one of the dogs I walked from the event to his transport back to our kennels. As I walked him, I held his leash with my left hand and leaned forward to offer my right hand to sniff. To my surprise, he jumped slightly, bumping my hand with his cool damp nose. I smiled and patted him.

"You're a shweetie bug, Rohan." I smiled, knowing it probably wasn't a term anyone had used to describe him before. When it was his turn to load, he leapt lightly into a crate perched in his transport van.

The second time I handled him at an event, he seemed to recognize me. Which wasn't that surprising because I'd spent about an hour with him at the last event. We did our loop around and around the mall. And I held my hand out for him to sniff. He seemed to like that and would hop to rise up to touch my hand with his nose. After three loops, we stopped again at our patch of grass. I tried talking to him again, wondering if this time I could break through his concentrated focus.

"What was your family like?"

Sometimes they were there. Sometimes they weren't.

"Did you like being an outside dog?"

Not sure what you mean?

"I heard you were outside most of the time. Not in the house with your people. So I wondered if you liked being outside?"

I liked the quiet.

"So in your new home, would you rather be an outside dog?"

Oh. I am neeevvveeer going through that again.

"I get it. What would you like in your next home?"

Nice. Quiet.

"What kind of people?"

Active. I have energy. But I do like quiet because then I don't have to be so focused.

"Yes. I agree with that. What else?"

Funny.

"You mean you want them to have a sense of humor?"

Oh...no...I want it to be a fun place.

"What is fun for you?"

I would like to fly through the air like other dogs I've seen.

Like a Frisbee dog?

I don't know what you mean by that.

"The dogs you see flying. Are they chasing a disc, a flat object, through the air?"

Then I saw a vision of Underdog. The classic cartoon character of a white-ish dog who flew through the air with a blue cape. They'd remade the cartoon into a movie a couple of years back. He must have seen it on TV.

"Ohhhh...you mean Underdog."

I don't know his name. But he flies. It looked like fun.

I smiled. "Underdog does good deeds. He helps people who are in trouble."

Good for him. I just want to fly.

I laughed. I knew he wasn't trying to be funny, but it struck me that way anyway. I didn't bother to ask Rohan if he'd be good with cats. It was clear that he wouldn't be.

Rohan got up and indicated that he'd like to walk on. So we walked around the mall again and stopped in front of PetSmart on a stretch of grass opposite the front doors. A guy rode by on a bike. Rohan went off in full-on attack mode. Sharp and incessant. Rah Rahw Raw Rah. Then he lunged at the guy. I gave him a quick but subtle verbal correction. "Ssshht!" I said and turned him in the other direction. He quieted. But it had startled me. I had heard about, but not seen, this side of him. And it all happened so fast. My heart beat a little faster, and I was slightly rattled by his aggression. But we continued to walk.

Later that day, he reacted the same way toward a couple of teenagers sitting on the sidewalk behind some bushes.

"He doesn't like guys on bikes…or teenagers either," I commented to Bart as we stood waiting to hand off our dogs to the van transports.

"Noooo, he doesn't," Bart agreed. "I heard that kids used to ride by on bikes while he patrolled his fence at home. They'd taunt him and throw rocks and sticks at him."

"No wonder," I said and then handed him to his transporter.

Later, I saw Sharon and told her what had happened. "I didn't correct him except verbally. Should I have done something different?"

"No, that's good" she replied. "He's a sensitive boy. He just needs to know that you'll protect him. You did the right thing."

The following week at our event, I walked him again.

And he was friendlier still. After our second loop, I saw Sharon walking another dog. Rohan saw her too. He locked her in his sights and whined. "Look who wants to come see you," I called out. She smiled and waved me over. Rohan lit up body and soul. His serious exterior melted, and he morphed into a playful puppy, jumping joyfully on her and play-bowing for her to chase him. "What would his family think if they could see this? He's a different dog, and that's just after a few weeks."

We parted ways, and I took Rohan on our typical loop around the mall and found our spot of shady grass. This time he lay down near me, and I stoked his fur and zoned out. He flipped on his back, inviting a tummy rub. I grabbed his sides with my hands, rubbing him vigorously. Then I shook him playfully. He leapt to his feet and play-bowed. I play-bowed back, drumming my hands on the soft turf. He grabbed my wrist in his mouth. I withdrew my hand, batted at him softly, and then shoved him. He pounced on me, knocked me over, and then rolled in the grass next to me. I laughed with joy.

Rohan had played! With me! It was a great honor to see him cut loose and suspend his constant vigil of scanning the horizon for danger. He sprang to his feet, and I did the same, and we dashed through the parking lot, then slowed to a walk. But the memory of that moment stayed with me as did the awe that it inspired.

A few days before the New Year, Caron and Vanessa and I decided to take three dogs for a field trip, so we met at the kennels. It was a beautiful, balmy winter day. The kind Southern California is famous for. Tess, our leader, had suggested we take Felice, Sophie, and Lagos. But I hadn't handled Lagos much. I don't know why I assumed I would take the male dog, but since I did, I requested Rohan instead. I knew he needed to get out. At the last event, someone else was handling him, so I wasn't able to spend much time with him, but even from afar, I could sense his spirit waning. Rohan will always have a streak of the wild in him, and he needed an adventure to feed his soul.

We packed the dogs in crates in Vanessa's SUV and headed for Daley Ranch, a wildlife preserve with miles of trails. Once we arrived, we unloaded the dogs, and I scanned the dirt parking lot. I had forgotten that Daley Ranch was a mecca for mountain bikers. This place was filled with cyclists.

"Well, this will be interesting," I said to Vanessa.

"What do you mean?"

"Rohan hates people on bikes."

We shared a knowing look and made our way to the trailhead, filled our water bottles, and set out. Rohan was on high alert. Senses acutely aware of the sights and sounds and smells that were new to him. I kept him close, knowing his distrust of people on bikes, strange dogs, and strangers in general. But he walked calmly, taking every new situation in stride. From time to time, he'd look up at me, and I'd offer him my palm, and he'd bump it with his nose. Each time he did, I smiled.

We'd been walking for about an hour and took a side trail. Two adolescent boys rode toward us on bikes.

Rohan's ears pricked, and I could feel his intensity mount. Adults on bikes were one thing, but these boys were replicas of the ones who'd chased and taunted him when he'd been guarding his property.

"Uh uh," I said.

His ears softened, but his focus didn't. The boys rode past us without incident, and we walked on. I patted his head and praised him. We stopped and took a break to appreciate the gorgeous backcountry. Olive-colored oaks clustered in tight bunches, and California holly clotted with bright red berries peppered the landscape. A half-dried pond choked with cattails moistened the trail's edge. A crow cawed in the distance, and a hawk circled overhead, stalking prey. I scratched the base of Rohan's tail, and he dropped his haunches a bit in response.

I knelt and offered Rohan some water from my bottle. He drank heartily, draining it. We walked on until we reached a picnic area. Several bikers and families sprawled on benches and fallen logs. In the distance stood an old, brown log house with spruce-green porch columns and a matching shingled roof. Further still, several weathered, red storage buildings stood abandoned and drunkenly askew on their foundations. We sat at a picnic table to give the dogs a break in the shade.

"Is there water here?" Caron asked.

"There used to be. Over by those sheds," I said, motioning to the storage buildings. Caron walked toward the buildings and searched.

"I can't find anything," she called.

I rose and started to walk toward her with Rohan. The same young boys we'd seen earlier rode up on their bikes. Rohan bristled. "Leave it!" I commanded and corrected slightly with the leash. His prong collar fell from his neck. I grabbed for it, but it melted away in my hands like thawing ice. He was free, and he knew it. He charged the boys, growl-barking. The nearest boy froze, dropped his bike, and then started to run.

"Don't run!" I yelled. I went out of body. No feeling, only reacting, all cells firing.

The boy hesitated and faced me. I continued to walk. Rohan barreled toward them. The boy turned to run again.

"Stand your ground! Don't run! Rohan! Come!" I continued to approach.

The boy grabbed his bike. Rohan was almost upon him now. The boy circled, using his bike as a shield to protect himself. Rohan snarled and circled fast, looking for an attack entry.

"Rohan. No!" I yelled. "Rohan! Leave it!"

Rohan broke his focus and looked toward me. Our eyes locked. *What am I doing? This is not who I am anymore.* It was more a feeling that came over me than actually hearing him say the words. I held my connection with his eyes. It was as though we were connected now through a portal of energy. "Rohan! Come!" Rohan galloped to me. I engulfed him in my arms, partially to contain him, partially to console him. He seemed shaken. As though he'd witnessed his own regression in the midst of the chaos and was confused and terrified by it. Confused by the old behaviors he'd reverted back to and terrified by the fact that he'd lost his cool so profoundly.

I struggled to reattach his collar, but I couldn't function. I had used all my energy to break Rohan's focus on the boy. "Caron," I said, "I can't do his collar. I need you to help me." Caron approached.

Vanessa called out to me, "Slip the leash over his neck. Do it like a noose until you get the collar fastened."

I'd already started to do this, but my hands and fingers fumbled. It didn't matter, I could tell Rohan wouldn't try to escape. He seemed relieved to be in my arms. I looped the leash around his neck and held his collar, but didn't fasten it until Caron was at my side.

"I can't believe he came to you," Caron said when she reached me. She grabbed the ruff of his neck to make sure we had him, while I fastened the leash around him.

"Me neither."

"He's obviously really connected to you or there's no way you could have recalled him."

"I think we were divinely assisted," I replied, as she struggled to fasten his collar. "I'm not sure this had anything to do with me. But for the record, I'm sooooo glad I connected with him these past few weeks."

Caron clipped his collar in place, and we returned to Vanessa, standing about twenty feet away with her dog.

"My god," Vanessa said as we approached. "Are you okay?"

"I think I'm a little shell-shocked," I said. "Rohan could have seriously injured that boy."

"That was amazing. I cannot *believe* you got him to come," she said. "What a good boy. Tell him he's a good boy."

"We were lucky," I replied. I knelt before him and took his face in my hands, pressing my forehead to his.

"You are such a good boy. I am so proud of you. You did such a good job. Thank you for coming back to me. Thank you, thank you, thank you, puppy." He buried his head in my chest and then licked my chin sweetly.

You're good for me. I believe in you.

"What made you come?"

You asked me to. You've taken the time with me.

Several more bikers converged a few feet from us, and a family with young children and two small dogs strolled past. Everyone went about their business as though nothing had happened. I thought it was odd that no one had sprung to our defense or offered help. They'd all just watched as though rooted to their spots. Another family approached with two young boys on bikes. Rohan eyed them nervously. I could feel his body key up. "Let's get out of here," I said. "We need to get him away from all this stimuli."

"Why don't we go to that far table," Vanessa suggested.

"I think I need to get him out of here altogether," I said. Then I looked over my shoulder and spotted a pair on horseback approaching. "Oh, God," I muttered and looked back at Vanessa and Caron, "Now! Let's go."

Vanessa looked around and saw the horses too. "Oh, shit," she said. "Yeah, we need to get him out of here." We headed south on a wide paved road, the main route back to the car, and then took a side trail that looped around the main route.

We stopped once more and sat in the quiet place, shaded by tall oaks. The female dogs in Vanessa's and Caron's custody play-bowed and barked. Rohan crouched and growled sternly. "Hey!" I growled back, my voice deep and gravelly. It broke his focus on the dogs. He softened and turned to me, licking my chin repeatedly. Vanessa and Caron chatted back and forth while their dogs investigated each other. I stroked Rohan's head, allowing myself to drift for a few moments. Finally, we rose and resumed our trek back to the car.

Three more bikers rode past us. Rohan lunged at the third, uttering a deep, guttural growl. "No!" I commanded, pulling him back. He stopped and walked on. But I sensed now that Rohan had had it, that he was saturated and almost anything would trigger his aggression. And I had lost my faith in his ability to rise above the chaos and hold himself together, which only compounded the problem. Whatever his behavior became now, I was responsible for it.

Three more bikers rode toward us. I corrected him with a light tug to break his focus before he could react. "Uh uh," I said. Rohan remained calm. "Good boy," I praised and patted his head. Another family approached walking two small dogs. Rohan was on alert. I corrected lightly. Again, he remained focused but quiet. I praised him again, and he looked up at me for reassurance.

We were almost to the car now. A couple approached. The woman pushed a stroller, and the man walked a chocolate lab. I kept my eyes on Rohan as we passed each other. Rohan locked the dog in his sights. "Uh uh," I said. But Rohan took offense. He lunged at the dog, going off in full attack. I tensed and braced against him. "Leave it!" I growled. He reared and lunged toward the dog. I pulled him off balance, and we walked on. We reached the car without further incident and loaded the dogs. I slithered into the front seat. Every fiber of me was exhausted.

We arrived at the kennels and started to unload the dogs. Felice and Sophie hopped out of the car willingly, most likely looking forward to dinner. I opened the back hatch of Vanessa's SUV, unlatched Rohan's crate, and took his leash. He didn't move.

We're back here? You've brought me back here?

I looked into his eyes and felt his sadness. I understood. Although our kennels are clean and comfortable and sound, it was like I was sending him to prison. I had shown him his freedom, and now I was returning him to captivity. I pressed my forehead to his and held him. "I'm sorry. I know. I wish there was more I could do for you."

There is no hope.

"There is always hope. All we have is hope. Don't give up. We will find you a family. There will be a home. Until then, I will be here for you." Tears welled in my eyes, and I stayed, arms wrapped round him for some time, then withdrew. He hopped out of the car.

The magnitude of that afternoon took days to process. I was off balance and off center, like a warped, melted record that has sat too long in the sun. A slew of "what-if's" swirled in my head, weaving together a complex tapestry of insecurities that would haunt me. When we bring a dog into Coastal's care, we give them a new name to symbolize a fresh start. What if Rohan hadn't been with us long enough to learn his new name? What if he hadn't responded to me? What if he'd bitten the boy? What if he'd done worse than bite him? What if I had been unable to stop any of it?

Caron and Vanessa tried to reassure me, tried to tell me that I was being too hard on myself, that I had handled the situation beautifully, that I needed to give myself more credit for creating the success. After all, they pointed out, it wasn't like I'd lost control of Rohan or let him off the leash. And they were already in motion to assist had things gotten further out of hand.

But because I hadn't had the next step mapped in my mind had my recall effort failed, I felt that I too had failed. I hadn't had a plan. I'm not sure whether you can have a plan in the midst of a chaos you've never experienced before. But I was badly shaken, as was my confidence.

When I emerged days later, into a place of peace, I reflected on the scene for the umpteenth time. The power of Rohan's eyes as they locked with mine in that moment of panic and chaos and recognition. The redemption I felt as he ran to the safety of my arms. These were moving mementos of an afternoon that could have gone awry in the worst way but hadn't. I went to Rohan later and asked him what he felt about that day.

It was catatonic.

"You mean before or after,"

I meant cataclysmic.

"For me too. What did it do for you?"

It made me aware of who I was.

"You did such a good job. I saw it in your eyes. That moment of revelation. It was one of the most powerful things I've ever witnessed."

I'm glad you were there.

"I'm glad too, but it scared me."

Me too. Intensely.

Would you want me to take you out again. By yourself?"

All by myself.

"Just you and me then?"

If possible.

In the weeks that followed, I spent more time with Rohan. He's changed a great deal since his first day with us. He's still keen-eyed and alert, but more out of observation than a desire to attack. He rarely barks at people, or bikes, or skateboards anymore. And while he has the occasional disagreement with a dog, those are less frequent as well. Still, he will be one of those who's not the easiest to place. People are drawn to him for his stunning classic beauty, but finding the right situation for him is a process that Coastal will not rush.

Since every Coastal dog I had connected with had taught me something, I wondered what Rohan was here to teach me. I closed my eyes and asked for an answer. What I heard was:

As above, so below.

Suddenly, I knew. Rohan's message is that we are all products of our environment. We become what we see modeled for us. We become what we are allowed to become. Positive and negative.

During his time with his family, Rohan became a guard dog. And he became good at it. But, improperly channeled, it led to aggression that would have made him dangerous. Had the cycle continued, he might have attacked, maimed, or even killed someone or something, and his people would have been powerless to stop it. Instead, his people realized that they could no longer handle him, so they relinquished him.

In Coastal's care, Rohan received socialization, leadership, companionship, structure, guidance, and affection. And he developed a completely different awareness and response to the world around him. His experience empowered him to manifest an entirely new persona. It was a graduation of sorts. As though he had completed an evolutionary cycle and, with that act, entered through a gateway and into a brand new existence. Rohan has broadened the scope of his own self-perception. His beliefs about himself and his environment have shifted, and as a result, his sense of self-worth and self-value will be ever expanding, in the most wondrous of ways.

Rohan was eventually fostered by John, one of Coastal's core members. John had recently adopted a female shepherd from Coastal so Rohan not only had a temporary home, but a foster sister as well. Rohan immediately thrived in the loving, yet rough-and-tumble environment, of John's bachelor pad. It was a perfect mix of comfort and mayhem for our high-octane boy. Each night, John's community turns the nearby golf course into a nightly dog park where neighborhood dogs enjoy romps and playtime with each other. It was delightful to think of Rohan playing with his peers for the first time in two and a half years.

John worked diligently with Rohan to address his many issues. He was a strong yet compassionate leader and in his care Rohan truly blossomed. But even in this environment, Rohan still faced challenges. One night, when John was entertaining guests, a young 20-something woman leaned into Rohan's space. She ignored Rohan's initial warnings and repeatedly attempted to kiss him. Rohan bit the woman in the face. You can imagine the chaos that ensued. Ambulances, hospitals, doctors, stitches, insurance companies, lawyers, and court hearings. The woman and her parents wanted Rohan declared vicious and were demanding that he be put down.

Tess and John leapt to Rohan's defense and attended his hearing and several meetings with police and animal control in an attempt to tell his side of the story. Rohan wasn't vicious, he was unpredictable.

I was beside myself. We all were. And I was disappointed that the young woman seemed unwilling to take any responsibility for her role in creating the situation. But as Vanessa so eloquently put it, our society doesn't take responsibility anymore. Everyone is a victim looking for someone else to blame. Fortunately, Rohan was found innocent and the young woman was found at fault.

I believe that if there is a lesson to be learned from Rohan's plight it is this; if you intrude upon an animal's space and choose to ignore their body language, what happens next is your responsibility, not theirs. Entering anyone's space, especially a stranger's, without coming from a place of innocence and love, puts everyone in jeopardy.

It's sad to me that humans think their rights are more important than the animal kingdom's. We don't own our planet, we share it. Everything we think we possess is actually on loan to us. And we, as humans would do well to remember that.

Severance

"I just heard Severance is coming back. Do you know why?"

"He's dog-aggressive." Vanessa answered.

"He wasn't aggressive when he was with Coastal."

"Yeah, but you can't always predict what behaviors are going to emerge later on."

"But they've had him for eleven months?"

"I know. It's a mystery to me too. Especially since the guy said he felt Severance was real close to turning the corner."

"Huh," I replied.

I first met Severance when he was just a year old. A beautiful, sweet, black and tan puppy with soft fur. Curved tear ducts in the corners of his eyes gave him a loving, kind expression. Caron had sent me several dogs to profile via email. Kerberos and Severance were in the same batch.

"What kind of home do you want?"

Big yard. Lots of plants and trees. I'd like it to be like a jungle.

"Are you good with other dogs?"

Yes.

Cats?

Not sure.

Kids?

I love kids.

Tell me more about what kind of home you'd like.

Lots of activity. I like to play.

"Anything else?"

He didn't respond, but I was shown a vision of a lush, tropical backyard with stately palm trees and dense shrubs and ferns. Deep teals and grass greens overlapped, creating exotic patterns of light and shade. A stream gurgled in the background, and a black panther slunk through low-hanging foliage, prowling the area. I wondered if Severance had been a panther in a previous life.

I shared the conversation with Caron, emphasizing that Severance seemed to be into his flora and fauna and told her I would see her at the adoption event on Saturday.

My daughter and I wandered into PetSmart amidst the din and chaos of the adoption event. I searched the crates until I found him and then opened his door and let him out. We took him for a walk, stopping behind PetSmart where it was quiet. I knelt, and he licked my chin heartily, like it was smeared with gravy. "What a sweetheart," I said.

"He *is* a sweetie bug," Hailey agreed, stroking his head. "I don't think he's going to be good with cats though."

"I don't either. But we can ask Casey if he has any background about how Severance is doing in his foster home. Maybe he's the one for us."

I followed up with Casey. He told me that Severance was living with a cat in his foster home and that he ignored the cat. This surprised me because intuitively I felt that he would have a prey drive. Three days later, Casey called me again. Severance was coming back to the kennels because he'd started chasing the cat. Turns out that during his first few days in his foster home, he'd had pneumonia. Once he started to feel better, he got a bit more interested in the cat.

The following weekend, I saw him again. He sat in the center of the adoption area, offering a paw and a kiss on the chin to the new people he met. He was adopted that day. And it seemed like a perfect fit. So we were all surprised when he was returned a year later.

When I heard Severance was coming back, I decided to cancel my plans so I could volunteer at the event that Saturday. I'd been so busy that I'd missed the last two events, and I felt guilty about not seeing Rohan. To be honest, volunteering had begun to take its toll. I'd spent a year of Saturdays with Coastal by now, and I was a little burned out. And aside from Rohan, I'd not really been able to create a special connection with any of our dogs, which fueled my apathy. But since Severance had been one of my favorites, I felt a bit more inspired to attend.

I stood at the door of the kennels, and Jess handed me a dog. "Who is this?" I asked.

"Severance."

I smiled, knowing there was probably a reason he and I were being paired today. It had been a year since I'd seen him so I didn't recognize him. I grabbed his leash, and we walked briskly through the crowd. Since he'd been labeled dog-aggressive, I wondered if he'd go off on anyone. But he seemed more intent on getting through the crowd. Maybe he was searching for his people in this sea of strangers. He strained at the leash, and I struggled to keep a firm grip on him.

We made our way through people and dogs without incident, and once we were safely beyond the crowd, we paused to greet each other. "Dog-aggressive my ass." I muttered. Then chided myself for being judgmental. I didn't know anything about him or his past. Maybe he only got aggressive when he was in his home environment or with people he was connected to.

I handled him for the next hour, and he never once showed signs of aggression. But he had no leash skills at all. I had to brace myself against his attempts to pull, so I began to wonder about all the training his previous owner swore he did with him. It seemed to me that Severance had spent little time on a leash.

We walked down a tree-lined dirt path, and I stopped in the shade to sit on a small concrete bench. Severance leaned into my leg for security, and I hugged his shoulders and rubbed him with my hands. His heart pounded. Poor guy was stressed. He licked my chin softly, and I stroked his fur and spoke to him soothingly.

"I'm sorry about all this stress for you. You must miss your home and your people."

I am worried.

"Try not to worry. We are going to do our best to find the perfect match for you this time. What did you like about your home?"

I had room to move around. And I loved the children.

"Do you remember the conversation we had when you told me that you wanted a yard that was like a jungle?"

No.

"Do you remember me?"

Vaguely. It's more of a feeling I remember than remembering you.

"Were you ever a panther?"

What's a panther?

"A big, black jungle cat."

I don't know. Maybe.

I smiled and then asked, "Were you connected to your people? I heard that your dad did a lot of training with you."

He didn't know as much as he thought he did.

Two more volunteers walked by with dogs. Severance watched intently but without any sign of aggression. I was puzzled. Why wasn't he displaying aggression? I decided to ask.

"When I knew you before, you were never aggressive. And today...I realize I've only been with you for an hour or so, but you don't seem aggressive. So why were you aggressive in your last home?"

I wasn't that bad.

"So you *were* aggressive then?"

Define aggressive.

"Fierce. Angry. Do you become that way when you connect with someone?"

I can have a tendency, but it doesn't always need to come out.

Suddenly, I knew what he meant. Many shepherds are this way. If they are with someone who can be a strong, confident handler or leader, there's no need for them to be in charge. But if they sense any weakness or indecision, they feel it is their duty to step up and take control of the situation. It's this trait among other things that gives them the reputation of being vicious even though they aren't.

We walked back to the event. Sort of. Severance half dragged, half power-walked me back. I found Jess so I could share my observations.

"Jess, I don't think he's dog-aggressive," I said.

"Oh, I know." Her tone dripped with disdain. Jess doesn't have a lot of patience in regard to humans. "He's *never* had an issue with the dogs in the kennels, and he didn't before he got adopted."

"I don't think his last family did much with him," I said, "He has no leash skills at all. Wouldn't a dog who's been with a family for a year know how to walk on a leash?"

She shot me a look of disgust and rolled her eyes. "They probably just left him in the backyard the whole time."

"Well, if that's the case, it's good that he came back. We'll find him a better match."

"Dobie!" Tess called out, "Who do you have?"

"Severance."

"I need him; this family would like to meet him. Can you bring him around to the side of my van?"

Severance and I took a circuitous route around dogs and crates and chairs. An attractive young couple with three darling young children waited for us. Tess opened the back door of her van and removed a small plastic crate housing a large tiger cat. She placed it on a table and called Severance. I gave him some slack but retained my hold on the end of the leash. Severance approached Tess but ignored the cat and tried to leap into the back seat of the van. She called him back and held the crate to his nose. He ignored the cat again. I was surprised. I had pegged him as being bad with cats. And he'd chased the cat in his first foster. I guess it just depends on the chemistry. Or the cat.

"See, this is what you want," Tess said. "See how he ignores the cat? He's more interested in us or in getting in the car."

After a few more thwarted attempts to get him interested in the cat, Tess gave up.

"Would you like to spend some time with him?" I asked. "We could take him for a walk." The woman nodded. I pointed to a destination and told them to meet me there.

"Do you live locally?" I asked when they caught up with me.

"No, we drove from Long Beach," she said.

"Wow, that's a commitment."

She smiled.

"Have you had a shepherd before?"

"No, but I love them. I've always wanted one."

"Did you come to see anyone specific?"

"Matrix, Rohan, and Severance."

I smiled. "Oh. I know Matrix and Rohan well. I wouldn't put them with someone who's never had a shepherd before. Neither is easy to handle. And neither is great with children. They're gorgeous, so I can understand your attraction, but Matrix and Rohan need to go to homes with experienced people. Severance, on the other hand, he seems pretty easy. Loves kids."

"That's what Tess said."

"Did she mention the dog aggression?" I asked, tousling Severance's ears.

"Yes, but we're willing to work with him," she said. "In fact I'm willing to do whatever it takes. We don't want to fail him."

They spent about half an hour walking, petting, and talking to him. Severance seemed to like them.

"Don't you wish you could tell what they're thinking?" the man asked, nodding in Severance's direction.

I smiled but said nothing.

"I mean it would be great if he could tell us if he wants to come home with us," he said.

"Even if he could speak your language," I said, "I doubt that he is in the frame of mind to make any decisions. He's still a little fractured over losing his family."

"Of course," she agreed.

The dad knelt, and Severance kissed him and offered his paw.

"Do you need more of a sign than that?" the wife asked. She'd made it clear awhile ago that she was already in love with our boy.

"So do you want to make it official?" I asked.

"I think we're ready," she said.

I walked them to the adoption table and introduced them to Verna to do the adoption contract and told them I'd wait and hold Severance. The sun warmed my shoulders as we waited. I felt his back from time to time to make sure he wasn't too hot. Another volunteer with a dog approached the water bucket near us. I watched Severance for a reaction. He wagged his tail, barked joyfully, and then play-bowed, inviting the dog to play. Yeah, he was dog-aggressive all right.

"Loose dog!" Someone behind me yelled.

Everyone was on the alert. A pale silver and tan female streaked past me. Those not handling dogs sprung into action.

"Don't chase her!" Tess shouted.

The dog darted into oncoming traffic amidst a chorus of screams and gasps from volunteers. My hand flew to my mouth. Tears welled in my eyes.

Charles and Bart dashed into the road waving their arms, hailing cars to stop. I held my breath and willed them to be safe. Tires skidded and screeched and three lanes of traffic came to a haphazard halt. The dog galloped back through the event, and several volunteers cornered her and placed her in a safe, secure crate. We all breathed easier.

Moments later, Severance's new family approached. They were beaming. "Are you ready to go home?" the woman asked and took his face in her hands. "Merry Christmas," she said turning to her children. Their eyes widened.

"Really?" they chorused.

"Yes, really. You didn't know?"

The girls shook their heads. I smiled, and we walked to their car together. I said a last goodbye to him, shook their hands, and thanked them. Severance jumped into the front seat of the truck, and they drove away, waving gleefully.

I walked back to the event and took Rohan out of his crate for a walk. He seemed happy to see me and kept looking up at me while we walked. Once past the clutter of the event, I knelt to hug him, and he jumped into my arms and licked my chin.

I was glad I'd made time to come to this event. It was good to see Rohan and share a few moments with him, and it had been awhile since I'd been that involved in an adoption for a dog I was connected to. It's the most gratifying thing you can imagine.

I went to Severance in his new home.

"How are things?"

These people are so kind.

His tone made me teary; there was such wonder in his voice. "I'm glad. You deserve it. How's the cat?"

He's okay. I pretty much ignore him.

"Good. Keep doing that. I'm so happy for you, puppy."

Thank you for that day. I was scared, worried. Terrified actually. You gave me hope. I believed you. I believed what you told me. And it happened.

"That's why I'm here."

Dogs you connect with are lucky. You restore their trust, their faith.

"I think a lot of our volunteers do that. Especially Jess and Sharon."

Maybe. But I felt that my world was falling apart, and somehow you made it better.

"Thank you, sweet boy. Have a wonderful life. You so deserve it."

I retreated and reflected on my experience that day. It was no accident that Severance and I had been paired at the event. Suddenly, I realized his purpose. I had lost my passion for rescue work. Our adoption events had become a series of Saturdays strung together one after another in monotonous perpetuity. Like a strand of synthetic pearls masquerading as the real thing, I was showing up but only going through the motions. My heart wasn't in it. And the dogs could probably tell.

None of us can be fully engaged unless we bring our hearts as well as our minds to the table for it takes both components to ignite the true power of passion. We must carry the belief in our minds, but it must burn in our hearts like a torch. Severance's adoption immersed me in the purpose of the rescue process again and reminded me of why I do this. He had assisted me in reclaiming my passion, and it was a special gift. Thank you for the nudge, beautiful boy. Thank you from the bottom of my heart.

Reagan

"Check out this girl's photo when I send it," Caron said. Her voice sounded tinny, and it echoed through the bad connection on our cell phones. "I'm sending you an email. I think you'll be perfect for her. She belongs to a friend of mine. A woman I work with. She's losing her house, and they can't keep their dog."

"I'll look," I replied, "but my life has become crazy busy since Legend was with us. I can't say 'yes' to a dog right now. I'm working so many hours, and I'm never home. It wouldn't be fair to anyone."

Caron sighed. "I figured that was the case, but I thought I'd ask. The reason I thought of you is that she supposedly loves cats."

I laughed. "For the record, Caron, when someone tells me their German shepherd loves cats, generally that's code for, 'they love the cat they grew up with.' All other cats are fair game."

"You may have a point, but, Dobie, I can't say no to my friend Nancy. She has nowhere else to take her. Maybe

I can just foster her until we find a good home. Can you come with me to evaluate her and do the meet-and-greet with Mandie on Saturday? I need an experienced handler with me."

"Of course. I'll leave Coastal's adoption event early, and we can go meet them."

On a stifling September afternoon, Caron and I piled Mandie, a crate, bowls, water, and blankets into the back of her car and headed out to meet Nancy and Reagan.

Caron craned her neck to see as she backed her red Rav 4 down her driveway, "I guess her one issue is that she's a little dog-aggressive."

"How bad?"

"I don't know."

"How old is she?"

"One year."

"So that means she's had a year to cultivate a bad habit."

"Well, not quite. Nancy has had her for eight months."

"That's still eight months of negative reinforcement. If she's dog-aggressive, what are you going to do? I mean, what about Mandie?"

"What *about* Mandie? *You're* the one that can talk to her. Why don't you ask her?" Caron suggested.

I quieted myself, tuned in to Mandie, and then replied. "I'm being told that Mandie will be okay if she knows it's just a temporary foster."

"Can you tell her that?"

"I did."

"Either way, I'm going to *make* this work," Caron said, "I have to. One way or another, that little girl is coming home to me."

I admired her determination. Maybe it was just my current stress level, but in her shoes, I'm not sure I could have committed to an indeterminate length of time with two dogs who might not get along. But I decided to look on the bright side. Maybe it would go well. Maybe the two girls would be fine together.

Caron's friend waited for us by a lake. I got out of the car and met Reagan. She was adorable. Friendly, sweet, beautiful, and a dramatically dark black and tan. Her face was almost completely black. And her bronze eyes were clear and sharp. She was petite and refined, probably about forty pounds if that. She needed to gain a little weight.

I offered Reagan the back of my hand. She lowered her ears, licked my hand, and wiggled into my arms. Nancy's son walked Reagan on a Gentle Leader, a leash that goes around the nose, designed for dogs that are pullers. I personally don't care for them because if a dog lunges and you try to restrain it, the device can jerk the dog by the nose and cause damage to the neck and spine. But there are other people who think this specific leash has merits. Caron approached and put a prong collar on Reagan and started to remove the Gentle Leader. My intuition kicked in.

"Let's leave it on," I said. "Let's attach the leash to the prong collar but leave that around her nose. If she gets aggressive, it will keep her from being able to bite Mandie."

"Good idea," Caron replied.

I walked Reagan for a few minutes while Mandie was still in the car to get a feel for her and get her used to the new collar. She backflipped a couple of times at the pressure and then settled. Caron opened the side door, and Mandie jumped out. They walked across the street. As soon as Reagan caught site of Mandie, the hair on her back bristled, and she lunged forward, barking at Mandie. I restrained her, and she backflipped repeatedly, trying to get away from me. I corrected her quickly with a light tug on her collar and a "shht" sound. We repeated this about ten times. Finally, she calmed. And I praised her.

Reagan and I approached Caron and Mandie. More barking and aggression from Reagan. Each time, I corrected her and then praised and patted her when she settled. Within five minutes, she calmed and walked quietly beside Mandie. They even shared a kiss. Then Reagan would revert to aggression, and I'd correct her again. This happened several times. Peace then aggression. Each time, I'd correct and then praise progress. Soon, she was leaning into me and looking to me to protect her. This little dog clearly needed the strength and support of a human leader. Her aggression was simply fear-based. Once she knew the human on the other end of her leash would protect her, the aggression dissipated.

Caron and I were astonished by her transformation in such a short time. Over the next ten minutes, she seemed happy to walk alongside Mandie. Even Nancy was amazed at the progress we'd made.

"I think she's going to be fine," I said to Caron.

Then I walked to Nancy and allowed her to say her goodbyes.

"Do you think they should leave first, or should we?" Caron asked.

"I think we need to leave first. Reagan shouldn't see her people walk away from her. She needs to leave them."

Caron opened the back of her car, and Reagan jumped up willingly and entered the crate.

"Caron, let's have Mandie ride in back with Reagan. It will be good for them to be side by side and get used to each other while they are safely separated."

Nancy came to the window and thanked us tearfully. I placed my hand on my heart, Caron grabbed Nancy's hand, and we both told her how sorry we were for her loss.

As we drove away, I said, "I know your friend is distraught, but this is for the best. Nancy was Reagan's friend, not her leader. And it's clear she doesn't know a lot about training or shepherds. In six more months, this girl would have been out of control and Nancy would have had no choice but to relinquish her."

"I have to agree with you."

"Caron, I hate muzzles, but it might be a good idea to get a muzzle for Reagan. So she doesn't start something with Mandie."

Caron agreed, so we stopped at a pet store to purchase one. I stayed in the car with Reagan while Caron and Mandie shopped. Reagan kept searching for Mandie. I thought it was a good sign.

We arrived home, set up a crate for Reagan, and introduced her to the backyard. She skirted the edge of the pool and then plunged her nose in the water.

"She's a water dog!" I said.

"No kidding. I won't be surprised if she dives in."

Suddenly, Mandie charged Reagan from behind, knocking her into the pool and almost sending me in as well. Caron pulled Mandie off, and I pulled Reagan out of the pool.

"If that happens again," Caron said, "walk over to the steps and coax her out. If she falls in, she has to know how to get out on her own."

"Right. I forgot. Sorry."

"What do you think started that?" Caron asked.

"I don't know. It surprised me too."

Caron went indoors with Mandie to get something to dry Reagan. She returned, handing me a towel. I rubbed Reagan dry, and Mandie charged her again. Caron lunged for Mandie, but her haunches slipped through Caron's hands. I growled at Mandie to stop and threw the towel over her head. Reagan hunkered between my legs and scrambled out of harm's way.

"Okay. We're going to have to keep them separated." Caron said, grabbing Mandie's collar and leading her inside.

"So much for my intuition," I said, slipping Reagan into the safety of the crate. "Mandie told me during the meet-and-greet that she'd be okay with Reagan."

We collapsed on Caron's leather sofas and sipped glasses of crisp, chilled Gewürztraminer.

"Mmm, this tastes so good," I said, swallowing the sweet, cold wine, "What a stressful afternoon."

"Ya think?" Caron said. She rolled her eyes. She slid lower on the sofa and rested her head on the back.

"How are you going to manage this week?" I asked.

"Like I said, I'll just keep them separated."

"Well, my hat's off to you. I couldn't deal with this right now."

"I'm not sure I can," she said, "but I don't feel I have a choice.

The next morning, I emailed Caron to see how things were going. She responded back that things were worse between Reagan and Mandie and that she had to keep them separated all the time. Then she asked me to speak to both dogs to find out what was going through Reagan's head, and she asked me to tell Reagan that she was sorry she had to be in a crate so much.

I quieted myself and went to Reagan.

"Are you all right?"

I feel alone and worried.

"I know. I'm sorry, puppy. Please try not to worry. I'm sorry you've lost your home, but we will find you a new home with good people."

I'm worried that I won't stay in this new home.

"We won't place you anywhere where you might come back. You'll only go to people who are able to work with you."

That's good to know.

"Caron wants you to know that she is so sorry that you have to be in a crate."

Oh. I am sooo clear about why I am in a crate.

"It's for your own protection."

I'm not afraid of Mandie.

"Good. You're a special puppy. I can tell. You are super smart. A rare blend of sensitivity and intelligence."

Thank you.

"Mandie is jealous of you. It's not because you are in her home. It's because you have an energetic sensitivity that she will never have. And she knows it. I'm not saying Mandie isn't beautiful or smart, but you have an evolved intelligence that is rare."

Then I went to Mandie.

"What's going on with you? This puppy isn't staying. I thought you said you could get along with her."

I can't tolerate her attitude.

"Lack of tolerance seems to be a theme with you."

She's sanctimonious.

"Are you sure you're not just jealous?"

Why would I be jealous of sanctimony?

I sighed. "Or maybe you're in denial. Mandie, just because Reagan has a capacity that you don't doesn't make you less than her. It's not about being better or worse; it's simply about being different."

Mandie retreated, and I couldn't reach her after that.

I reported back to Caron via email. I told her how sorry I was that I wasn't able to take Reagan myself and suggested she reach out to Sharon to get her to come evaluate Reagan's aggression.

The following day, I had an email from Caron. She'd met Sharon and Sharon's dog, Sedona. Reagan had been great with Sedona. So now we knew that with a calm, accepting dog, Reagan would be fine.

Caron brought Reagan to the next adoption event, and within thirty minutes, a family was interested in her. Sharon approached me at the end of the event and asked me if I could foster Reagan for a few days.

"This family will most likely adopt her early in the week," she said, "but their one concern is how she is with cats. If you take her, it would give us a chance to see how she behaves with kitties."

I was still crazed at work, but I couldn't say no to Sharon. She does so much for Coastal, and she was asking only for a few days of my time. People may wonder why I don't foster more often. Fostering is easier for some than others. Since we don't have a fenced yard or other dogs, it's a commitment to make sure our new foster doesn't take off when we're outside playing and to make sure that they get appropriate exercise. I can't just open the door and let them play and run off all their energy. And the cats almost always seem to be an issue—even with dogs who are good with cats—because my cats don't know how to stand their ground. Their lack of confidence seems to entice dogs to chase. But I said yes, and Reagan came home with me.

She hopped into the back seat of my car, and I reached around to give her a pat before we took off. Poor little thing had had so much stress in the last week and to top it off had attended a rescue event where she was surrounded by other dogs. She was handling it well.

Or not. At the first stop light, she hunkered down and let loose an explosion of diarrhea on my back seat.

Then she promptly hopped in the front seat with a look that said, "*I'm* not riding back there."

When we got home, I let her out and kept an eye on her while she explored the yard and I cleaned the back of my car. Then I boiled rice and chicken to add to her food in hopes that it would ease her digestive trauma.

She was a lively little thing, so I took her outside, grabbed several tennis balls, and stood in the midst of our long sloping driveway throwing ball after ball. She dashed back and forth with the speed of a greyhound, and we played until she was worn out. Then I led her back inside and introduced her to the cats. She was great with them.

The next morning, I asked for permission to bring her to the ranch where I board my horse, Bear. Several Labrador retrievers live on the ranch, and I felt that the more Reagan could be exposed to other dogs and schooled in appropriate behavior, the better. While you're not typically supposed to throw a bunch of new and stressful situations at a new dog right away, I felt intuitively that I needed to build on the experience Reagan had had at the adoption event sooner rather than later.

We were still in the truck when she saw the ranch dogs for the first time. The hair on her neck bristled as soon as she saw dogs in the distance, and she barked aggressively, but all it took was a few corrections and a supervised meet-and-greet with her on the leash and she quieted. One dog in particular, Daisy, who belonged to another boarder, didn't seem to like Reagan and curled her lip during their meeting, but all the others accepted her and ambled peacefully away to lie near their people.

On the way to the arena, we walked past several other labs in a dog run. They rushed at us, barking and growling aggressively. Goose, a big white male, tried to jump the fence and failing that, he grabbed the chain link in his teeth and tugged fiercely. Reagan's hair stood again.

"Uh uh," I said, "you don't need to engage in that." To my surprise, she followed my queue and ignored them. I walked her past them several times to continue the desensitization process. The labs barked ferociously. I kept talking to her. She kept her eyes on them but didn't engage. I praised her profusely, and she leaned into my leg with soft ears and soft eyes.

I led her into the arena and let her off-leash. She sprinted to the far end to see the horses. Her little paws thudded softly in the deep sand. She turned and raced back to me, then dashed away again. I could feel her sense of wonder as she took in all the new sights and smells. Daisy, the dog who hadn't liked her, squeezed through the slats of the arena gate, and Reagan galloped toward her. I froze for a split second and thought, oh my God, either this will end in a blood bath or Reagan will get a good lesson in socialization from a canine teacher. I was about to call her, but something stopped me.

The memory of what happened next will remain with me forever. Reagan play-bowed. Daisy mimicked her, and they dashed around the arena chasing, jumping, and tumbling each other. Reagan took her cues from Daisy's body language, and for the first time in eight months was playing, running, and socializing with her peers. It was one of the most beautiful things I had ever seen. So much joy. Such pure delight. My heart soared, and I was moved and privileged to have witnessed something so completely innocent, joyful, and awe-inspiring.

Reagan was adopted the following Saturday, and Caron and I met the new family to do the handoff together. They are wonderful people who understand shepherds and will be perfect for Reagan. They even have plans to adopt a young male lab from another rescue so Reagan will grow up with a playmate. They have a huge fenced yard for exploring, a cat, and an iguana. Their eldest daughter is a runner, so Reagan will have plenty of opportunity to burn off steam.

She hopped in the back of their van and lay down on a soft sky-blue sheet while Caron and I talked to the woman and her daughter. When it was time to say goodbye, I walked toward her. She rose to sit position, and I took her face in my hands, kissed her nose, and told her goodbye.

When I got home, I didn't immediately clean up after Reagan. I didn't pick up the balls she'd scattered through the yard and house. I didn't toss the bits of napkin she'd shredded. I didn't empty her water dish or wash her food bowl. I wanted reminders of her for awhile. Because I didn't cry before she left. This time, I cried after.

A dear friend who'd met Reagan at the ranch asked me how I could let her go since it was obvious that I'd bonded with her. It was quite simple: the other family was a perfect match for her. I owed her that.

I went to Reagan after her adoption.

"How are things going?"

It's amazing here. There's lots to see.

"How's the iguana?"

He's spiky.

I laughed. "And how do you get along with their cat?"

It's nicer than yours.

I laughed again. "Do you miss your original family?"

It was a home, not a family.

"What's the difference?"

Families live together.

"You didn't live with them?"

Not always. There's something you must know.

"Tell me."

Being with you was like being in a constant state of grace. You brought out the best in me. My time with you allowed me to become what I had intended to become.

Her message overwhelmed me. I knew I had been a good influence on her, but I had no idea of the full impact of my time with her. A few moments passed while I let her message sink in. Finally, I responded. "Thank you, puppy. I am honored to have played a role in that. You are special, and your new people are lucky."

I knew Reagan for only two weeks. But in that time I watched her evolve from a fearful, aggressive—albeit sensitive—pup into a confident, secure, and brilliant little girl, which was exactly what she had intended. As she indicated, I may have helped to facilitate her growth, but all I really did was offer her the opportunity; it was she who did the work. Because of this, she will go on to live a great life. This time, she will have a family, not just a home.

Oprah Winfrey once said that the choice to be excellent begins with aligning one's thoughts and words with the intention to require more of one's self. I believe this is true. Intent invites us to dive bravely into the deep pool of personal transformation, where we may all be reborn and therefore usher a newly formed expression of ourselves into the world. The ability to adapt and re-adapt to life's situations allows us to grow, expand, and evolve. Every situation is a necessary component in the construction of our present and future reality. When individuals commit to the process of self-expansion, they become cloaked in such brilliance that self-doubt and insecurity are impossible. And it all begins with intent.

Annika

Angels come in many forms. Sometimes with four legs and fur. Like Annika. A sensitive female with a bunny-soft, cream and black coat and the fragile energy of a deer. Her tender, tentative kiss and deep, gentle eyes spoke to her enormous capacity to trust and love and hope, even though life had not been kind.

Annika was a stray. Abandoned by her people, she wandered the streets for the better part of two years. Scrounging for scraps to stay alive. Dodging people who didn't want her in their yards or trashcans. With little food to nourish her, she'd dwindled to 45 pounds. About half her required weight. Hip bones the size of doorknobs pushed through her coat like those of a starving cow in third-world country. Every rib was visible.

When we first met Annie, she was lying in a cramped, narrow dog run, one of many in this particular animal shelter. Almost hidden from view under several other dogs, she lay resigned and hopeless. Sometimes it takes one angel to rescue another. Annika's first angel of mercy was Jess. Jess handles the first leg of the rescue work, salvaging dogs from high-kill shelters and bringing them into Coastal's care. And she recognized the beautiful potential of this fragile creature.

Annika was ushered to the secure shelter of a crate in the back of Jess's van. She sniffed, circled clockwise, and nestled under a soft down comforter. Then, she tucked her nose under her tail and fell into a deep sleep.

In Coastal's care, Annika was given as much food as she could eat to restore her health and vitality. But soon, her caregivers recognized that this alone would not be enough. Eating triggered severe diarrhea and vomiting. And despite constant feeding, she wasn't gaining weight. Coastal dug deep, searching for a solution.

In time, they found a specialist who had treated similar cases and was able to diagnose her issues. Due to Annie's emaciated state and prolonged periods with meager food, she had developed a digestive complication called EPI. Her pancreas had shut down, and without it, she couldn't process food.

The answer was a pancreatic enzyme, added to her meals, as well as a battery of other medications. At several hundred dollars a jar, the pancreatic enzyme wasn't cheap and had to be mixed with the food and water in just the right way. If it was too dry, it wouldn't work. If it was too wet, it would eat away at her mouth and make it bleed.

Two of Coastal's core volunteers, the same couple who had fostered Valiant, stepped in to foster her so Annika could regain strength in their tranquil home. They monitored her eating and meds, took her to weekly weigh-ins, and loved her back to health. Finally, she was ready to enter the adoption circuit. And was snatched up quickly. But the alpha female in the new home started to bully Annika. For her welfare, she was returned to her first foster home.

When she was stable again, Caron contacted me and asked me to foster Annika to see if we could be a match for her. They thought that because I could communicate with her I'd be perfect for her. I thought so too.

But we were wrong. I was no match for Annika's physical issues. I couldn't figure out how to mix her food right, and her bloody mouth stained the water in her dish pink. It killed me to think I was causing her pain. And I was overwhelmed by her medical regime. I stressed. She stressed more. And we fed off each other, creating a vicious cycle.

Days passed, and the change and stress ate at her. Her body was shutting down, and I could feel it. She stopped eating. And I panicked. She couldn't afford to lose weight. I was failing her. I wasn't equipped to deal with her issues.

After many tearful phone calls, we decided that Annika should return to her previous fosters for her best interests. She could tell something was afoot. That another change was underway. I tried talking to her to assuage her fears. I tried to tell her that she was simply going back with her fosters. People she knew and trusted. People who loved her. But my words couldn't sink in. She was blocked with fear.

I transferred her on a dreary, rainy December morning. She wouldn't get out of my car. Maybe she didn't want to get wet. Maybe she didn't want another change. Finally, she unwillingly gave in and hopped dutifully into the back of Sam's jeep. She stared blankly into my eyes and said, *You too?*

I winced. And my heart tightened. I knew what she meant. She had put her faith in me, and I was abandoning her, like others in her past. I started crying. Foster mom Holly put her arms around me. But she cried too. She'd had to give Annika up twice. She knew my pain.

Once they got Annie home, she settled in and raced around her familiar home, stopping only to plant joyful kiss after kiss on her foster parents' cheeks, knowing all was well in her world.

While she was in my home, I had asked her about her past.

"How long were you on the streets?"

As far back as I can remember.

"How did you find shelter?"

I slept under bushes. One in particular.

"What happened to your people?"

They got tired of me.

"How could anyone get tired of you?"

There was a new puppy. Named Thumper. They thought he was cuter. They stopped noticing me. One day I just slipped out the back gate.

"And they didn't try to find you?"

I don't know.

"What did being with us mean to you?"

Healing.

"You or me?"

It is like a staircase.

"What is like a staircase?"

Healing. We place a toe on a stair and then another toe. Step by step, we climb out of the darkness.

Silence settled over me and then the realization that she was right. I still had remnants of sadness in regard to Blitz, but for the most part I was healed. Months of denial and then grief and pain had finally given way to acceptance. One by one, these dogs had assisted me in climbing out of the darkness—the womb of grief. Now I was truly equipped to go forward and help others heal. Especially the shepherds who had given me so much.

Annika was adopted in late February of 2009. To a wonderful family whose gentle kindness was a mirror of her own. Annie now has two beautiful children in her life to love and nurture, as they will her. After three years of searching, Annika found her forever home.

I've thought about Annie a lot since meeting her. And I think I came into her life to help her process some of the emotion she'd amassed in her short lifetime of pain, and heartache, and disappointment with the human race. I had spent most of the time Annie was with us in tears, unable to cope with what had happened in her past. I couldn't bear the thought that anyone had ever been unkind to such a gentle and loving spirit. And I held harsh judgment about whoever had first abandoned this girl and anyone since who'd caused her pain. And while I believe that every situation has an up side, I struggled to understand the good in what Annie had endured.

One day I stumbled upon a passage in a website. Seemingly out of nowhere. It's message—that when we see pain and suffering and grief, we must remember that it is only the tip of the iceberg. A minute speck in the totality of the universe. And that if we were only able to see the big picture, we would witness a complex tapestry of joy and pain, of good and evil, of triumph and failure all woven together in perfect harmony. Such is the yin and yang and the ebb and flow of life. It is how we learn lessons, grow, and evolve.

No matter what has happened in the past, our experiences—bad and good—allow us to live again, to laugh again, and to love again, more deeply than before. It was then that I understood Annika's purpose—she is a gentle teacher, reminding us to love in the midst of pain, to have hope when all seems lost, and to forgive those who have hurt us.

She invites us to expand our awareness, to live life with a higher purpose, and to inspire others to do the same. Her dream is that one day our global human consciousness will evolve to the point where there is no abuse or neglect, where ignorance will be stamped out, and as a result, our world will be transformed. Until that day, angels like Annika will continue to be the change they want to see in the world.

Afterward

I'm still searching for my German Shepherd. After
two years with Coastal, I still haven't found "the one."
Perhaps if I had found my perfect dog I would never
have come to know the others as deeply as I did. And
I might not have spent the past two years in service to
Coastal German Shepherd Rescue, nor would I have
reaped any of the rewards or lessons, or felt the love,
joy, sadness, and healing that I experienced. Perhaps for
now I'm not meant to have just one dog. Perhaps for
now, they are all supposed to be mine.

About
Coastal German Shepherd Rescue

Coastal German Shepherd Rescue of Southern California is a non-profit 501(c)3 public charity dedicated to finding loving homes for abandoned German Shepherds in San Diego, Orange, Los Angeles, and the Inland Empire.

Coastal is dedicated to providing new beginnings for homeless German Shepherds who have been abandoned, neglected, abused, or relinquished by their owners to local shelters to await an uncertain future.

Coastal is committed to finding loving permanent homes for the orphaned dogs in their care. Coastal is an all-volunteer, non-profit organization whose mission is to educate the public about German Shepherds, their lifespan, personality, activity level, along with overall responsible dog ownership while working diligently to match each dog with the appropriate adoptive family.

At Coastal, it's all about the dogs.

For more information about Coastal and our dogs visit www.coastalgsr.org

For more information about Finding Forever—The organization, visit www.findingforever.org

About the Author

Dobie Houson is an experienced writer, researcher, consultant and communicator. For twenty-six years Houson has served as Director of Corporate Communications and Director of Marketing Research for Ken Blanchard and The Ken Blanchard Companies, best known for writing and publishing mega-bestseller, *The One Minute Manager*®. Her expertise has helped the organization brand and differentiate itself as an industry leader in training and development.

As the founder of Finding Forever, and a part time animal communicator, Houson is a passionate animal lover and has a desire to understand and connect with them more deeply. She has trained with intuitive counselors and animal communicators for over a decade, honing her skills and in turn teaching others. Houson has owned and trained dogs and horses. Her experience with dogs in general, and specifically German Shepherds as well as horses, gives her insight into the way animals think and behave.

Most recently, Houson has been published in *Why We Ride*, an anthology on women and their connection with horses, as well as in *Chief Learning Officer* magazine and in the *Human Resources Development Review* journal. Houson is also the founder of StrategiCreation, a consulting firm that provides strategic planning, marketing, communication, and branding solutions for startup companies allowing them to identify and brand their niche and create a compelling vision for the future.

Houson is a graduate of California State University Chico, where she received her degree in communication. Houson lives in Valley Center, California with her family, two cats and a horse.

Made in the USA
Lexington, KY
06 March 2011